G000060021

DISRUPT

AND

CONQUER

To
Dr Kumar

[signature]

3/6/18

With warm regards

[signature]

ADVANCE PRAISE FOR THE BOOK

'An excellent narrative of an accidental businessman building a diverse conglomerate amid adversities. T.T. Jagannathan's story resonated well with me as it captures the trials and tribulations that every entrepreneur has to undergo while building a differentiated business with the potential to touch millions of lives across the globe'—Kiran Mazumdar Shaw, CMD, Biocon

'I have known T.T. Jagannathan for the last thirty years and he continues to impress me with his knowledge and ability. While several companies have keeled over when faced with adversities, TTK has reinvented itself and marched ahead to greater heights. The turnaround story of the TTK Group is one of India's great success stories!'—N. Vaghul, former chairman, ICICI Bank

'This book celebrates with elan the extraordinary life and times of T.T. Jagannathan, whose uncanny acumen and ability to predict, innovate, disrupt and recalibrate markets have deservedly earned him his flagship company TTK Prestige and the TTK Group in particular, and, more generally, a legendary status in the annals of Indian corporate history. He is a visionary leader, heading a consumer durables company whose products permeate most homes across India and the world, and what shines through is the tenacity and audacity with which every adversity is transformed into an opportunity to create a new success. It is a richly nuanced life story that exemplifies the indefatigable human spirit and the resultant triumph of labour, most worthy of accolades and, undoubtedly, of emulation'—Venu Srinivasan, chairman, TVS Motor Company

'It is delightful that business leaders can narrate their stories of struggle, success, mistakes and moments of glory. Jagannathan has an inspiring and instructive story . . . well told'—R. Gopalakrishnan, author and corporate adviser

DISRUPT
AND
CONQUER

How TTK Prestige Became
a Billion-Dollar Company

T.T. JAGANNATHAN
WITH
SANDHYA MENDONCA

PORTFOLIO
PENGUIN

An imprint of Penguin Random House

PORTFOLIO

USA | Canada | UK | Ireland | Australia
New Zealand | India | South Africa | China

Portfolio is part of the Penguin Random House group of companies
whose addresses can be found at global.penguinrandomhouse.com

Published by Penguin Random House India Pvt. Ltd
7th Floor, Infinity Tower C, DLF Cyber City,
Gurgaon 122 002, Haryana, India

Penguin
Random House
India

First published in Portfolio by Penguin Random House India 2018

ISBN 9780670090174

Typeset in Adobe Jenson Pro by Manipal Digital Systems, Manipal
Printed at Replika Press Pvt. Ltd, India

www.penguin.co.in

MIX
Paper from
responsible sources
FSC® C016779

CONTENTS

INTRODUCTION

The simpler an innovation, the greater its elegance.

They call T.T. Jagannathan India's Kitchen King. Acknowledged by his peers, his colleagues, the media and, most importantly, the market, for his brilliant business acumen, Jagannathan steered the spectacular revival and repeated turnarounds of the south Indian conglomerate TTK Group, and its flagship company, TTK Prestige.

Not only has he revived the fortunes of a storied third-generation group of businesses, he has also invented the Gasket Release System, the first of many product and process innovations in his thirty-five-year career, which has made cooking and kitchens safer. At seventy, Jagannathan is still innovating new cooking systems, such as the world's first microwaveable pressure cooker and microwaveable coffee maker.

Be it a cooker or a condom, somebody someplace close to you or halfway around the world is at this moment using a TTK product. From cookware to babycare, snacks, pharmaceuticals, heart valves, prosthetics, deodorants, maps, mops and more, the TTK conglomerate operates in thirty different categories. Its popular products are available in every continent.

The TTK Group was founded in 1928 in Madras (now Chennai) by T.T. Krishnamachari, who later became a Union minister and held the portfolios of finance, industry and commerce for close to fifteen years.

Soaps, chocolates, pens, clocks, cosmetics and condoms . . . the TTK Group was among the earliest to introduce several such Western goods in India, building up a vast network of distributors. Close to 150 products of the major multinational companies of the time came to India through TTK: Sunlight and Lifebuoy soaps, Beecham and Cadbury, Kraft cheese, Kellogg's cornflakes, Sheaffer pens, Aqua Velva aftershave lotion, Horlicks, Maclean, Enos and many more. And then it lost them all.

Over the years, the Group has built powerful brands of its own, tenaciously gaining not just a pan-Indian but global market for many of its products. The Group now has a turnover of over Rs 2400 crore ($378.6 million) and a market capital of Rs 10,000 crore ($1.57 billion), and includes two publicly listed companies, both of which are cash-rich, a remarkable phenomenon in itself. TTK Healthcare Ltd has several verticals, including pharmaceuticals, foods and personal care, and with the merger of a group company, it also makes condoms. Its current market capitalization stands at Rs 645.35 crore ($101.8 million).

The Group's flagship company is TTK Prestige, India's largest kitchen appliances company. With a market cap that exceeds Rs 9400 crore ($1.4 billion), it is one of the top 500 listed entities in India.

Like a phoenix, the Group and its constituent companies have risen from the ashes, many times over, to stand tall and proud. This is the story of a journey that began with early success and met with catastrophic disasters, then saw the company turning its fortunes around in stunning comebacks, again and again.

Disruption has been its key characteristic; it disrupted markets and its own nature of business to meet challenges and triumphantly conquer them. This is the story of its 'mission possible'.

What makes this story all the more startling is that the billionaire businessman T.T. Jagannathan, who steered it through this journey, is an accidental and reluctant businessman. He came into the profession very unexpectedly, and without any preparation, with neither an MBA nor any work experience in the family business before having its very survival thrust on him.

TTK Group Structure

T.T. Krishnamachari & Co. is a partnership firm and the holding company for:

1. TTK Prestige Ltd, a listed company in consumer durables, making pressure cookers, cookware and appliances.
2. TTK British Holdings Ltd & Horwood Homewares Ltd, part of the UK Subsidiary of TTK Prestige Ltd.
3. TTK Healthcare Ltd, a listed company in pharmaceuticals, medical devices, consumer products and foods. TTK

Protective Devices Ltd, which makes condoms, was merged with the healthcare business in December 2017.

4. TTK Services Private Ltd, which provides services to non-resident Indians and does knowledge process outsourcing.

5. Cigna TTK Health Insurance Company Ltd, a health insurance JV with Cigna of USA; TTK is set to exit the JV after regulatory approvals in 2018.

Sandhya Mendonca

1

AN ACCIDENTAL KING

Learning to define a problem
helps you find its solution.

'You need to come home now. The family business is collapsing, you have to come back and do something to save us.' These unexpected words, uttered on a beautiful spring day of 1972 by my father, at a restaurant in Ithaca, changed my life forever.

It was certainly not the life that I had envisaged for myself when, armed with a gold medal from IIT Madras, I set out to live my dream in Cornell University, savouring the world of academia. As things came to pass, I was pitched from the calm environs of a university campus into the roller-coaster world of business. I vividly recall the day it all started.

Destiny comes calling

Cornell was at its best in the spring. I love Cornell any time of the year, but spring did put a pep in my step. I was just about twenty-four, soon to get a master's degree in operations research, and had landed a great job, when my parents came to visit.

I met them at the small airport in Ithaca. They stayed a week at a hotel close to my apartment, as my mother thought my place was too filthy. The day before they were to leave for home, the three of us sat down to dinner.

The conversation that followed changed the whole course of my life. Destiny takes us on paths that we have never imagined for ourselves. Enjoying a carefree life in America, I was far removed from the turmoil and chaos that had gripped the family 13,000 kilometres away in Madras. The family business that was started in 1928 by my grandfather, T.T. Krishnamachari, was sinking.

As we finished our meal, Father told me, 'You need to come home now. The family business is collapsing, you have to come back and do something to save us.' My first, and incredulous, reaction was, 'Why is it in trouble and why can't you or Paapu [my older brother, Ranganathan] handle it?'

I had always assumed that as the eldest son of the family, Paapu would take over the business from my Father. This had influenced my choice of becoming an academic. But Father said, 'He's not going to do that. You have to come and help.' A second revelation followed: Paapu had become an alcoholic and was in no condition to run the business. And my younger brother, Raghunathan, was far too young at that time.

I refused. I had never taken any interest in the business. I had not visited even one of the twenty factories that we had. I told Father, 'I cannot do that. I am an engineer. What do I know about business or marketing or finance? If you can't solve the problems, how do you expect me to do it?'

The emotional pitch

Father's reply cut to the heart. He had joined the business when he was just seventeen and had to deal with a series of crises. Now, at fifty, he was wearied of it.

He did not compel me to return when I refused to. 'We are asking you to come. It's up to you,' was all that he said. My next move was to invite my parents to come and live with me in America. I had just landed a job at Rand Corporation, and would start work after the summer holidays, but I was sure I would do well and be able to look after all of us. I told them in all earnestness, 'I am doing very well here and I can support you.'

But Father's reply was sobering, 'We owe a lot of money. Money that belongs to the depositors. These people have put their life savings with us and there's no way that I am going to leave the country and come away.' His attitude was very different from that of some of today's business people, who up and leave their responsibilities, escaping liabilities without a care for their employees.

Father was clear that he wouldn't leave Madras and the unpaid debts behind. 'No, we can't leave. If you won't come, that's it.' It seemed that there was nothing that I could do except return to India.

I realized that I could not keep refusing my parents' request to return, but I was also reasonably sure that whatever the problem was, it could be sorted out without too much trouble and I would be able to go back to Cornell. I had completed only two of the required four years for the doctorate that I had worked for. Man proposes but God disposes, and I had to leave America without my doctorate. (Twenty years later, Cornell gave me a doctorate.)

I was so sure I would return to the US that when I followed my parents to India, I left all my belongings—clothes, bags and books—back in the US. I was optimistic that I would be able to figure out what was wrong, help Father tide over the crisis and have the business back on track. How naïve I had been to think that, and how little I knew about the mountain of problems that lay ahead!

Shanthi Ranganathan, wife of the late T.T. Ranganathan, TTJ's older brother, recalls, 'Jaggu was completely devoted to his parents.' Latha Jagannathan adds, 'Jaggu has a strong sense of responsibility, and that made him stick to the commitment that his parents wanted from him—to rescue the family business.'

Defined by IIT

Indian Institute of Technology, Madras (IIT M) defines who I am today, as my experiences as a student there have influenced me the most and in a lot of ways. For one, I was brought up in a household where we children thought we were kings. In IIT, nobody is king. All your rough edges get smoothened off when you start living with people who treat you like they treat everybody else. You start learning how to mix with people as an equal. That was an important learning experience for me. The second change was the move from an air-conditioned room with a fancy bed to a small room with a steel cot. I got used to that too.

Many people can't handle the pressure and stress at IIT; I too struggled during the first six months and wanted to quit. But my mother advised me to stick it out for a year at least. I am very competitive, and when I decided to heed my mother's advice, I took to my classes like a duck to water.

I blossomed here. Until I came to the IIT campus, I had never come first in anything, though I was among the top scorers in school. I topped my IIT class that year, and topped everything in all my five years on the campus. After I scored the highest marks in class during the first two years, my mother made up her mind in the third year itself that I must get the gold medal in the final year. That did put pressure on me.

I gave up playing the violin to focus on my studies. I was very fond of the instrument and had earned a diploma from Trinity College of Music, London, with a gold medal. The violin is a very difficult instrument, though, and requires regular practice; one can't play it intermittently. Before I joined IIT, I had to make up my mind as to whether I would continue with the violin or not. I chose academics over music.

I thrived in the campus. From being an introvert, I became an extrovert, and my leadership qualities were honed during my stints as general secretary of the students' body and captain of the tennis team. And in my final year, I did win the gold medal, much to my mother's joy.

Inspiration

I had made up my mind to get into IIT in the summer of 1963. I was fifteen. This decision was influenced by a chance meeting

I had with four young men on a train ride to Madras from Delhi, where I had spent the summer with my grandfather. I was very impressed with the confidence and the manner of speech of my fellow passengers, and when I found out that they were students of IIT Madras, I decided straightaway that I wanted to join the institution too.

I prepared for a whole year, getting coached after school. I came fifty-ninth in the entrance exam. My coach was Shankar Iyer, who was to later start a successful coaching centre for students aspiring to join IITs. My fundamental understanding of mathematics was very good, thanks to my high-school maths teacher, Shiva Ramakrishnan.

I was born in Madras and had schooled first at Presentation Convent in Church Park and then at Besant Theosophical High School. My pre-university course was at Jain College. I was among the top 10 per cent in the SSLC exam, but the prestigious Loyola College rejected me, even though my uncle, T.T. Vasu, was a trustee of the college.

In my third year at IIT, the principal of Loyola College had been invited as the chief guest for the hostel day celebrations. In his speech he said all the toppers at IIT were from Loyola. I got up and said, 'No, I am sorry. I am the topper here, and I am not from Loyola because you did not give me admission.' I have to admit I enjoyed that moment.

Enjoying academia

Having taken to campus life, I set my sights on America. I liked everything about academia, and my plan had always been to become an academic and stay in the US as a professor, as teachers' salaries were very paltry back then in India, even in IITs.

While at IIT, I applied to several top universities—Cornell, Harvard, Yale and Princeton in the US, and Miguel in Canada, to study industrial engineering (IE). While the IE department is part of the mechanical engineering department in most colleges, in Cornell it was part of the operations research (OR) department. I didn't know what OR was and had to go to a library to look it up. I realized that OR was the subject I had wanted to study all along, and not IE.

It also helped that a very close American friend, Randy Lortscher (we are still friends and visit each other), who had spent three summers with my family in Chennai as an exchange student, had a sister, Martia, in Cornell.

Living in the US in the seventies was a daunting prospect as it was hard for Indians to get foreign exchange; there were no credit cards or easy access to telephones in those days. I was apprehensive of being all alone in a new land; thus Randy's offer of an introduction to his sister was very welcome and convinced me to choose Cornell. Martia's boyfriend, Tom Ragonetti, took me under his wing, even setting me up on my first date.

Defining the problem

I have never regretted the decision to join Cornell. It is a great university, with the most beautiful campus I have seen, and I enjoyed studying and living there. I later sent all my three sons to study there.

I enjoyed operations research; it was pure maths, and very different from mechanical engineering. The transition from

being an engineer to becoming a mathematician was difficult
initially, but very soon I became a straight-A student. In fact, my
probability professor, Brown, used to give me his tests before
giving them to anybody else. He would pose about twenty
questions, and if I answered fifteen right, he would tell everybody
else to answer just ten of the questions. And he would give me
an 'A' even before I took the exam.

What impressed me most about Cornell was its method
of education, which was very different from those in Indian
colleges and universities, including IITs.

In India, they teach formulas, based on which you make
calculations and work out the answer to the problem you are
asked to solve. In India, we don't define the problem, but only
find solutions to it. In the US, they want students to figure out
the problem itself.

Geniuses from India go to America to study because the
Americans are very good at defining the problem that is to be
solved. In Cornell, I learnt the importance of defining a problem,
and this has helped me throughout my life.

A famous classmate

At my first school, Presentation Convent, I shared a desk with a brilliant and pretty girl who later became a successful film star and went on to become the chief minister of Tamil Nadu: J. Jayalalithaa. We were classmates for five years, from classes one to five—from age five to eleven.

At that age, boys are not interested in girls, at least they weren't in those days. But I remember she was brilliant at her studies and very pretty too. I met her only once after that, at a family wedding, perhaps a dozen or so years ago. She was the chief minister of Tamil Nadu and had come there with heavy security. She saw me with the wedding party and sent for me. She asked if I remembered her and I replied that I did, of course. That was the extent of our interaction.

India's premier institute

The Indian Institutes of Technology (IITs) are premier engineering and technology colleges funded by the central government. These 'institutes of national importance' were started after India became independent, to nurture a new breed of technologists who would help the nascent nation's growth. IIT Madras was among the earliest to be instituted, IIT Kharagpur being the first.

Over the years, the number of IITs has grown from five to twenty-three, owing to the demand for seats. Each year, over 12 lakh students sit for the highly competitive IIT-JEE (joint entrance examination). A couple of lakh students succeed in this exam and take up the advanced exam, vying for the 11,100 seats (2017 figures) available at the IITs. The intense competition for entrance to IIT has led to the growth of several coaching centres across India that prepare students for the tests, and this industry alone is valued at several crore rupees. The coaching business is so lucrative that one centre could even afford to gift a new BMW car to a successful student!

TTJ, a campus celebrity

S. Ravichandran, who had a twenty-five-year career at the TTK Group before retiring as managing director of Prestige in 2015, recalls, 'I was two years junior to TTJ at IIT Madras. Both of us studied mechanical engineering. He was in the 1970 batch and I was in the 1972 one. I knew him because of his roaring Jawa bike on which he rode out of the campus zone. [Jawa, a very popular Czech motorbike brand, was built and sold by the company Ideal Jawa of Mysore; the Jawa 250 was a popular model.] It could be heard when he left his hostel, Jamuna, and passed my hostel, Narmada, which was the last. Later he bought a car, a VW Bug (Beetle), which didn't make as much noise, but we all knew when he was going out.

'He hasn't changed one bit from those days, he still has that effervescent, outgoing personality—jovial, loud, enjoying life at any point in time . . . that kind of personality. He is an absolute extrovert and loves people. He was the same even on campus, though I didn't know him personally, as I was his junior. But all of us there knew him, and knew when he was in the campus.'

2

THE FOUNDING FATHERS

It's never enough to start a business on a great idea;
the implementation has to be monitored.

Brutus says in Shakespeare's *Julius Caesar*, 'There is a tide in the affairs of men, which, taken at the flood, leads on to fortune.' This is true of the way my grandfather came to establish the TTK Group. Father and I also made the most of the opportunities that came our way, moving with the ebbs and flows of the tide.

Looking back, I feel that throughout my life everything that has come to me has come by accident, and that all that I have done has been by accident too. The pattern of accidents can be traced back to the very beginning of the TTK Group.

My great-grandfather, T.T. Rangachari, was a lawyer who went on to become a district court judge in British India. Before he attained this position, he was one of the 'Triplicane Six', the six young men who joined hands to start *The Hindu* newspaper in September 1878. They started it to counter the other, British-owned, newspapers in Madras, which were at that time disparaging of the appointment of an Indian as a judge in Madras High Court.

Over time, Rangachari went on to focus on his legal studies and became a luminary in the field. Not surprisingly, he wanted his only son, T.T. Krishnamachari (TTK), to become a lawyer too. But after graduating from Madras Christian College with a degree in economics, TTK did the unexpected and joined an indenting business owned by A.R. Doraiswamy Iyengar. The son of a high court judge taking up trade raised many an eyebrow, apart from the fact that it was still rather unusual for Brahmins to get into business when they were meant, hereditarily, to focus on learning. To silence his critics, Krishnamachari decided to work without pay.

Revolutionizing distribution

The business retailed soaps and oils, and over time it was appointed as the sole indenting agent in south India for the biggest British company names in those days, Lever Brothers and Beecham. Krishnamachari was keen to learn the agency business and proved to be so good at the job that when Doraiswamy's health began to fail in 1926, Krishnamachari began managing the business. When Doraiswamy died in 1928, impressed by TTK's efficiency, Lever offered him the south Indian agency, and thus, in 1928, was born T.T. Krishnamachari & Co.

Were there any indications that TTK & Co, which had an accidental birth, would grow to be the conglomerate that it is today? Perhaps.

Though he came into the business serendipitously, Krishnamachari soon showed that he had a keen sense for selling and significantly expanded his business. He travelled to distant towns throughout south India, and his excellent communication skills helped him establish a vast network of dealers across the hinterlands. This was a prescient act, and one that continues to contribute to the success of the TTK Group to this day.

With the insights gained from his travels, Krishnamachari came up with an innovative idea—'redistribution'. He set up his own warehouses, creating a distribution network that involved dealers across south India. Doraiswamy had followed a simple practice of booking orders from dealers for various goods and passing them on to Lever and Beecham. But it was impossible in those days to reach out to two million retailers, the bulk of which were mom-and-pop stores, from a central warehouse. India can be rightly called 'a nation of retailers'.

Krishnamachari made a crucial change in the earlier practice by appointing key distributors in each town to handle the redistribution in their areas. These distributors were in charge of logistics and ensured that the small stores that dotted the country were able to sell the soaps and oils TTK sold. Their local distributor could fulfil supply orders even if a small store wanted only a couple of bars of soap. With the implementation of this redistribution system, products began to reach more retailers, and orders increased substantially.

The system was revolutionary at that time, and the distribution patterns followed by FMCG companies in India— both multinationals and Indian companies—are based on this redistribution model pioneered by TTK. Lever continued the system put in place by my grandfather, and when it decided to handle its own distribution, TTK's sales manager,

R. Ramaswamy, moved to Lever Brothers, where he rose to become vice chairman of Hindustan Lever.

Krishnamachari went from town to town, getting town criers to popularize the merchandise he sold, persuading shopkeepers to stock his goods, and pioneering point-of-purchase displays, among other daring marketing techniques.

From 1928 to 1940, TTK & Co. continued to add more products to its portfolio, including Sunlight and Lifebuoy soaps. Krishnamachari found an effective way to ensure their presence and recall in every home by distributing calendars printed with images of gods and goddesses alongside the Sunlight and Lifebuoy logos. There was not a single home, perhaps, that didn't have these calendars in those days. So simple and effective was this idea that modern branding and advertising strategies pale in contrast.

From entrepreneur to politician

By the late 1930s, TTK developed an interest in politics and discarded his expensive suits for khadi and homespun cotton. He was elected to the Madras Legislative Assembly as an independent member, and subsequently to the Central Legislative Assembly from Madras in 1942, having defeated a powerful candidate from the Congress party.

He later joined the Congress after being influenced by Rajaji (C. Rajagopalachari, a Congress leader, who was then the chief minister of Madras state and became the last governor general of India). Rajaji became TTK's mentor, and introduced his brilliant protégé to Jawaharlal Nehru; TTK and Nehru became firm friends from then on. This friendship is significant for the impact it was to have subsequently on the Indian economy.

TTK next joined the Constituent Assembly, which consisted of eminent Indians and was tasked with drafting the Constitution of the soon-to-be-free India. Its deliberations from 1946 to 1950 culminated in the framing of the Indian Constitution. In 1948, Krishnamachari joined the Drafting Committee. There is a rare handwritten copy of the Constitution of India, signed by all the seven authors, in the TTK Group library in Chennai.

Brilliant, though arrogant, there was much that TTK achieved in national life, and it merits a book on its own. Suffice it to say that while his political growth was a matter of great happiness for the family, it wasn't quite so opportune for the business he had started. As events that would transpire much later showed, trading his suits for khaki was not a mere wardrobe change for Krishnamachari. The person who had set up a thriving business would become an unexpected and implacable obstacle to the growth of industry in India.

In 1939, TTK began to become more involved in politics. He handed over the reins of the business to his eldest son, my father, and from that day onwards completely cut himself off from the commercial aspects of TTK & Co.

My father, T.T. Narasimhan, was the eldest of TTK's four sons, and the burden of the business fell on his young shoulders when he was just seventeen. His studies were cut short after the intermediate level (the equivalent of plus-two) as the business demanded all his attention.

Maybe he had to undertake the task too young and without sufficient preparation, but he displayed an affinity for selling, and briskly went about building the enterprise.

A series of disasters

TTK & Co. had done such a good job of marketing Lever products that the British company felt it no longer needed a middleman. It decided to handle the distribution itself and dispensed with the agency. This was a rude shock to our company as it depended substantially on its earnings from the Lever business, grossing about Rs 75 lakh a year from it. The loss was cushioned to some extent as TTK & Co. still had the agency for Beecham and Cadbury's.

Close on the heels of the loss of distribution rights for Lever products came the Second World War, which hampered exports from the United Kingdom. There were no products coming into India, and for TTK & Co., whose indenting business wholly depended on distributing imported goods, those were very bad times indeed.

Business was at a standstill all the way until 1946. It had not been a hugely profitable enterprise to begin with. It had always run on borrowings, and in bad times Father borrowed more money as the agency had to pay its employees. Loans began to accumulate.

Things started improving from 1946, when the American firm Seymour appointed TTK & Co. as its agent in south India. Henry Seymour & VA Dodge represented several American firms such as Pond's, Kraft and Kellogg's in India. After Henry's death, his son, Lawrence, set up his own agency in Bombay (now Mumbai) in 1945 and appointed TTK & Co. as his agent in the south.

As a result of its relationship with Seymour, TTK introduced almost every major multinational company's products into India in the mid-1940s. It distributed over 150 products, such as Kraft cheese, Kellogg's cornflakes, Sheaffer pens, Aqua Velva aftershave lotion, Horlicks, Maclean and Enos.

Perils of power

Disaster struck the company again, and hard. This time it happened through the hand of T.T. Krishnamachari himself. He had been appointed minister for commerce and industry in Prime Minister Nehru's Cabinet in 1952. At that point in time, India was critically short of foreign exchange, and the commerce minister banned the import of consumer products that were considered non-essential.

This cut at the core of the Group's business, whose essence was to import consumer products and sell them in India. Grandfather had explicitly forbidden Father from visiting him in Delhi, so there wasn't much hope in our lobbying the commerce ministry.

'Necessity is the mother of invention', and truly this maxim can be derived from experience. The consumer products the Group sold—processed foods, oils and creams—had a huge market in India and the agency had an impressive distribution network to sell these goods. The only things now missing were the products themselves. And the only way out, decided Father, was to start manufacturing the goods in India. From merely distributing, TTK & Co. now also became a manufacturer of consumer goods.

In yet another instance of Grandfather's political position hurting the family business, TTK & Co. lost an opportunity to distribute Amul dairy products. In 1952, when Krishnamachari became the Union commerce minister, he imposed a 25 per cent cut on imports of butter to help the Kaira District Co-operative Milk Producers Union (popularly known as Amul, an acronym of the institution's earlier name, Anand Milk Union Limited). In an unrelated development, Dr Verghese Kurien, head of Amul, had zeroed in on TTK & Co. to distribute Amul products. But Krishnamachari was furious when advertisements announcing the distributorship came out in the newspapers as he felt his action of reducing dairy imports would now be seen as a move to favour his family's business. He announced in Parliament that if indeed the distribution rights for Amul had be given to TTK & Co., it was cancelled with immediate effect. Though he had no authority to do so, Grandfather cancelled the distributorship and lambasted poor Father over the issue.

This was a double blow as by curbing imports of food products, he had already adversely affected TTK & Co. But Grandfather was impervious to the harm his actions were causing his sons' business.

Making in India

The curb on imports marked an important milestone in the life of TTK & Co., and had major ramifications for its sustained growth.

Father had taken over as managing director of LD Seymour & Company in 1953, and this gave him the opportunity to meet with many American manufacturers directly. These meetings sparked the idea for TTK & Co. to venture into manufacturing, a big step from distribution.

Waterman's inks, Pond's face powder, Woodward's gripe water and Prestige pressure cookers were the first four products the company started to manufacture. Some were taken up under licence and some under joint ventures.

The companies borrowed heavily to set up factories, and repayment pressures followed. The gestation time for an industry is quite long, and the first five years are especially tough as payments are not easily collected. By 1959, the business had built up huge losses. These losses were weighing down the Group even after its companies started to return profits.

The looming debts, however, did not curb Father from going on a terrific expansion spree during the course of the next decade. Even as he went about starting businesses and factories at a rapid pace, the crucial area of operations was neglected. He was a true Sagittarian in his appetite for risk, and had a great ability to think far ahead of his time. The flip side was that his thoughts often soared high, and away from the ground reality.

Take, for instance, how he started making condoms, pharmaceuticals, hosiery and more. India had never heard of condoms until T.T. Narasimhan thought of importing them in the mid-1940s. He began by importing Durex condoms from London Rubber Company and, in 1963, set up a joint venture, the London Rubber Company (India) Ltd, to begin manufacturing condoms in Pallavaram in Madras. This was much before the era of family planning, as my father believed India needed condoms.

He set up Orient Pharma Private Ltd (now known as TTK HealthCare) in 1958 to manufacture Woodward's celebrated gripe water; this was an extension of TTK Group's activities in the field of pharmaceuticals. Beginning in 1953, it had taken up the distribution agency from pharmaceutical companies and, in 1958, got into processing and manufacturing too.

Father felt India desperately needed maps, and set up a new company, Maps and Atlases, in 1965 in collaboration with Bertelsmann of Germany. Next came Tantex, which Father founded in 1969 at Thanjavur under TT Investments & Trades Pvt Ltd to manufacture men's innerwear. With sales of Tantex soaring, he set up TT Textiles at Nagari, in Andhra Pradesh, to manufacture cotton yarn for the hosiery. Then followed the manufacture of TorToys in collaboration with Krupps of Germany.

Father also set up a big factory for yet another new business, Chemoleums, in the 1960s. This, again, was modernistic, and fits in with today's drive towards repurposing. Chemoleums took used oil from industries and refined and cleaned it for industrial reuse. But the problem was that back then nobody wanted to reuse cleaned oil because oil was very cheap.

Many of the products that Father started manufacturing were trailblazing for their times. Take the Waterman business, for example. Father had started Right Aids Orient in 1951 to make fountain pens and inks. He added ballpoint pens too, but his decision was thirty years too early since there was no demand for such pens at the time, and he stopped their manufacture. Who knew then that ballpoint pens would become such a hit?

Steve Jobs once said that people don't know what they want, and you have to tell them what they want. And my father was like that, he could see what people wanted. From ballpoint pens to maps and atlases, from pressure cookers to condoms, people in India wouldn't even have known what these products were at the time but for him.

A general without lieutenants

While all the new businesses were driven by progressive thinking, their execution was not very sound. Father was a great 'ideas' man. However, it's never enough to start a business on a great idea; the implementation of the idea has to be monitored. He also lacked a good team. If he had had a capable person to help run his businesses, he would have been one of India's biggest businessmen. But he lacked management skills, and this proved to be his Achilles' heel.

Some businesses require long gestation periods, but they work out in the end. If father had been funded, I would have become one of the top 100 richest people in the world. But he wasn't funded, and the Group couldn't bear the losses that began mounting.

Slowly, each of these businesses started making losses and contributed to the loss of Rs 10 crore that the Group had accumulated by 1970.

By 1972, the company was in deep turmoil. As the various businesses continued to make losses, the banks would not lend money. Father turned to the market (private moneylenders), and got finance at an usurious interest rate of 40 per cent. That made things even worse, and a downfall was imminent.

Things could certainly not go on this way, and neither could Father. The weight of the business had been his to bear since he was but a teenager, and it was wearing him down. It was time for me to shoulder my part of the responsibility, to pick up the baton.

The man who never harmed anybody

My father, T.T. Narasimhan, was a self-effacing man, and while he was always nattily dressed in white trousers and shirt, with a belt and a tie, you wouldn't notice him if he was in the room. He was very uncomfortable when I asked him to speak at the inauguration of the Hosur factory.

He was very affectionate but not demonstrative. He was more of a touch-me-not, and though Mother would hug us, he never did. It's very unlike how I have been with my children, hugging and kissing them from when they were born.

He helped a lot of people without anyone knowing about it. In later years, he would sit with my secretary and sort out what to do for the people he wanted to help. They would discuss it for hours at my secretary's desk outside my office, and even I wouldn't know what they were planning. He would pop into my office to say, 'I'm leaving,' and be off. If a book was to be written about him, the title would be: The Man Who Never Harmed Anybody.

3A

A THORNY BATON

I never sell at a loss. I would rather not sell at all.

What awaited me in Chennai was catastrophe, and one of such magnitude that I thought there was no way I could fix it. My first instinct was to sell the entire business for a single rupee.

If you ask me to look back and try to piece together the story of how things fell apart so badly, I cannot isolate a single cause that led to such a downward spiral. There was a string of decisions and outcomes that combined with circumstances to bring the TTK businesses to the sorry state that I found them in when I came back from the US.

While TTK was regarded as a great brand across India, the Group's net worth was negative at the time. There were twenty companies engaged in a variety of businesses, and except for one, none was in a healthy state. The Group was running on borrowed money, and its combined debts at the time amounted to Rs 10 crore (equivalent to about Rs 1000 crore today).

Hoping to sell the business, I went to Bombay and, along with Ajay Thakore, a tax consultant who was a director of TTK Prestige, met many people, but nobody was interested in taking on a debt-laden company.

Had the same situation existed today there would be a thousand bidders. But in those days, consumer products were not considered important. Steel, aluminium and cement far outweighed hair oil, toothbrushes and soaps. As a consumer products company, we did not interest investors at that time.

Mapping the turnaround

When the attempt to sell the business failed, I decided to rebuild the Group, one company at a time. I started with Maps and Atlases, as it was our biggest loss-maker at the time. We were losing Rs 60 lakh a year from that company in 1972. That's more than Rs 60 crore in current times.

If there are problems on many fronts, it does not help to fiddle a bit in each of the problem areas; the correction would take a very long time and sink you in the process. So I picked the worst of the bleeding companies, Maps and Atlases, and in two years I turned it around. It took pure common sense to fix the problems in that company.

Maps and Atlases Publications Pvt. Ltd was set up in 1965 in collaboration with Bertelsmann of Germany, one of the biggest publishers in the world and the biggest for maps and atlases. Bertelsmann held 51 per cent of the company and TTK Group, 49 per cent.

The Germans had methodically calculated that India, with 800 million people and 300 million children, would need

60 million atlases and 300 million maps a year. Strangely, even today, not even one million atlases are sold annually in India. This is not only because Indians share books, but it is also because students don't study geography thoroughly, which is critical for a proper understanding of the subject. The only maps that sell in India are outline maps, and we sell tonnes of them.

Father, as usual, had thought thirty years ahead of his time when he set up a factory in Pallavaram on a scale that could handle the huge volume of projected sales. But sales were not even a fraction of the projection, and the company was going bankrupt. Bertelsmann saw the writing on the wall and exited the business in 1972 by selling it to Father for Re 1. Father had guaranteed all the loans as the banks would not accept foreign guarantees. By 1974, the loan burden of Maps and Atlases was around Rs 2.5 crore, even as the press continued to incur losses.

On my first visit to the Mill (for some reason, the printing press was referred to as 'the Mill'), I found a terribly sad sight. It was such a huge factory, of around 2,00,000 square feet, but all the machines were lying completely idle.

Pivoting to print

When I took up the task of rescuing this company, I handled it in a very simple way. The first thing I did was to switch the focus from maps and atlases to printing. The logic was very simple; we had to get the business to start making money. I figured out how to price our products and went about generating business.

I came up with a rate card in a simple manner too. I worked out the P&L for each printing machine, how much it cost us and how much we needed to make. It was easy to calculate the rate card once I knew the costs per sheet for a 3000-run or 6000-run, for two-colour or four-colour. I entertained myself by doing these calculations in my head (these days computers give such data).

We didn't have a sales team, and I went around on sales calls myself, asking for orders. (At twenty-four, you can do things that you can't contemplate doing at seventy.) We took orders to print all kinds of things: books, pamphlets, posters. We printed school books for the Tamil Nadu government, we printed posters for the Congress party . . . we took on any job we could get. As TTK was in the consumer products business, we knew practically every advertising agency, and we approached them and got a lot of work. But it was not enough to turn the company around. Though we began earning revenue, it was not enough to make a profit on, let alone recoup the accumulated losses with.

But I came up with a second idea that helped the company, and I am happy about it even today. I suggested that we replace the labels on Woodward's Gripe Water, a popular digestive product for babies that TTK had introduced to India in 1928. We had started manufacturing it under licence in 1959. The Gripe Water packaging was a distinctive blue wrapper, and it consisted of a big piece of paper that was folded many times over around the bottle before a label was stuck on to it. This led to a lot of wastage of paper, time and labour. The paper was sourced from a mill in Punalur, where workers were on strike quite often, leading to delays in paper supply.

I suggested to Father that we could reduce the size of the wrapping paper. We needed only one-sixth of the quantity of paper we were currently using to wrap the bottles. We could also print the blue colour on white paper and print the label for the package. The staff at the Woodward's factory were worried. The product catered largely to the lower middle class, and the staff were apprehensive that customers would not accept the change in the product's appearance. They were in a state of panic, imagining it would harm sales. Resistance to change is endemic; I have experienced it many times in our various operations, and still do so.

I insisted, and quite strongly, on the change, leaving the staff with no choice but to accept it. We started printing the blue wrapper with the label in large volumes, leading to a sizeable reduction in procurement costs. With the additional work of printing the blue wrapper, all the machines were operating whole-time, in three shifts.

TTK Pharma (which runs the Woodward's Gripe Water business) continues to use the same system for labelling. The paper is being procured from another printer after we ceased the printing operations of Maps and Atlases.

Getting lucky

There was a time when Lady Luck came to our rescue, helping us get a new four-colour machine for the press. Maps and Atlases was still losing money, but it had enough work to feed another four-colour machine.

I had heard that one such machine was lying at the Madras port as the customer who had ordered it from Planeta in Germany had not been able to pay for it. After some bargaining, I brought the price of the four-colour machine down to Rs 6 lakh.

The bank was prepared to give me Rs 2 lakh, but I was still short of Rs 4 lakh. The man who is now famous as the chronicler of Chennai, S. Muthaiah, had then just left Colombo, where he was the editor of *Colombo Times*, and was working with us at Maps and Atlases. Muthu and I sat racking our brains for some way of coming up with the money.

Meanwhile, Father had gone to the races, where he backed two horses that won him Rs 4 lakh. He asked us to collect the money from the bookkeepers and buy the machine. Getting this machine was a turning point for the press, and it started making profits. I learnt printing technology in our press and worked on the machines too.

It is ironic that Father had initially resisted my decision to tackle the Pallavaram press. He had the notion that anybody who tried to run that company would be defeated, even destroyed. He seemed to view the press as a bull that killed every matador who faced it, and he feared for me, as if I were going to tackle such a bull.

All this while, as a general manager at Maps and Atlases, I was getting paid a paltry salary of Rs 800 a month. When I got engaged, I couldn't afford to buy my fiancée a sari, forget a ring, from my salary. I had turned my back on far more lucrative offers in the US and had come home, and I certainly expected a comfortable livelihood. But the senior management hit me with a whammy when they cited a provision in the Companies Act that meant that as the son of the chairman of the company I could not be paid more than Rs 1000 as an executive.

When I was appointed as managing director of TTK Prestige, (then known as TT Limited), my salary rose to a princely sum of Rs 5000. There's a funny story about this.

The managing director was permitted a maximum salary of Rs 5000, but this was subject to government approval. The old-timers in the company were cautious and wanted me to apply for a salary of Rs 2500 as they doubted the government would approve a higher amount. Ajay Thakore, feisty as ever, had insisted that I should apply for the maximum amount allowed. He was determined to fight it out in court if it was not approved. I applied, and it was sanctioned.

Learnings in England

We had some memorable meetings and setbacks too. There was a gentleman called Parthasarathy in Oxford University Press, one of the largest publishers in England at that time. He advised us to get OUP's printing business. We were competing with British printers, and we got all of OUP's business in Madras. Our sales calls also took us to the UK, to pitch to another publishing company, Longman. It was in a village called Hadham, and we took a train from London. I was particularly taken with the names of the Hadham towns—Hadham, Much Hadham and Little Hadham.

We were picked up at the railway station and taken on a tour of the area before lunch. We spoke generally about printing before heading back to London in the evening. But no business was discussed. We were to go back the next day to do that. When we did so, to my shock, I discovered that a Japanese delegation of six had also come to get the same business.

And this was the way it worked: I would give my quotation. The Japanese officials would be told that my quotation was cheaper than theirs. And then they would speak to each other in Japanese, although they could understand when John (the English client) and I spoke in English. Only one person from the Japanese team was authorized to speak in English. During this transaction, whenever I lowered my quotation the Japanese would lower theirs further, and thus they ended up getting the business.

Not only were their prices lower, but the Japanese firm was well known, whereas we were an unknown press. I learnt later that the Japanese increased their prices after six months. But I could not have lowered our price any further.

I have had that policy for my business my entire life. I won't sell at a loss; I'd rather not sell. Even today, even for orders of huge numbers of pressure cookers, we don't sell at prices that will not make money for us.

We ran the maps and atlases business profitably till 2015. With the advent of Google, a major portion of the business died. We sold the building, plant and machinery, but retained the title of TTK Maps, as they came to be rebranded, with us. We continue to sell maps and atlases under this name, but we outsource the printing. It's a very small part of the Group's business.

Though we were able to turn Maps and Atlases around, in hindsight we realized that we should never have got into the printing business. There is an old saying: 'If you are a publisher, then you should never have a press.' You tend to start publishing books that won't sell in order to feed the press, and then it becomes an unviable situation. Very few publishers have their own printing presses. The mistake we made was to set up a printing press instead of getting our maps printed by other printers. There were enough printers to print the quantities we required.

I had by then spent two years in India. When I had returned from America I had felt that I wouldn't survive more than a year here. I had not been inclined towards business, nor did I know anything about it. The complete trust that my parents placed in me kept me going through these difficult times.

Common sense to the rescue

What helped me turn this loss-making company around? I did not know anything about managing a business. It is astonishing that people don't realize the value of common sense and hard work. I went to work at 8 a.m. and worked till 10 p.m. I was there every day until night, making sure the machines were running. If they weren't running, I had to figure out the cause.

Business is a lot of common sense, which is indeed the most uncommon of qualities. You don't need highfalutin MBA degrees to build a business, though I do value the professionals with MBAs in our company. Take the examples of all the successful leaders in Indian business: Narayana Murthy, Kris Gopalakrishnan and Nandan Nilekani.[1] They don't have fancy

---

[1]   Narayana Murthy, Kris Gopalakrishnan and Nandan Nilekani are three of the seven co-founders of Infosys, the global technology services and consulting company, which is one of top ten most-valued companies in the Indian stock market.

     'Infosys Limited, Infosys—Company History & Defining Milestones', www.infosys.com/about/Pages/history.aspx; 'Infosys Back among Top 10 Companies by Market Cap on BSE, NSE', *Livemint*, 23 August 2017, www.livemint.com/Money/Jde6apyzP81RJ4xltl71EP/Infosysback-among-top-10-companies-by-market-cap-on-BSE-NS.html.

business degrees; they are all engineers. Azim Premji[2] is not even an engineer. If you take a look at the founders of digitally driven companies like Flipkart, Big Bazaar and Ola, none of them has an MBA. They have still done a great job.

Whether you have an MBA or not, it is important to be focused and to work hard. Narayana Murthy once said something that has really stuck with me as it reflects my life. He said, 'The harder you work, the luckier you get.' It does work that way. Luck comes your way if you work hard.

Twin births

Both Infosys and Wipro (headquartered in Bengaluru, like TTK Prestige) set out on their IT journey in the same year, 1981. And both Prestige and Hawkins began manufacturing pressure cookers in 1959, when the technology entered India.

---

[2] Chairman of Wipro, Aziz Premji left Stanford to take up the family business of vegetable and refined oil manufacturing at the age of twenty-one. He led the company's diversification into several consumer segments, and most famously into IT. Wipro is a leading global information technology, consulting and business process services company, valued at $7.7 billion as of June 2017.
Anthony G. Craine, 'Azim Premji', *Encyclopædia Britannica*, Encyclopædia Britannica, Inc., 17 July 2017, www.britannica.com/biography/Azim-Premji; 'Azim Premji.' *Forbes India*, www.forbes.com/profile/azim-premji/.

Wedding bells

Along with the glimmer of hope for the Group kindled by the successful turnaround of Maps and Atlases, on the personal front too, my life turned rosier.

As I had left home at sixteen to join IIT and had moved to Cornell from there, I didn't have too many friends in Madras. At the end of the one-year period that I had allowed myself to set right the family business, I realized there was a lot more to be done and that I could not leave India.

With the hours that I put in at the printing press, there was not much time to socialize, and in any case, what was a twenty-six-year-old to do in Madras? Dating there was out of the question; a chaperoned dinner with a girl while I was in IIT had set off such tremors that it was impossible to think of dating as Madras was still a conservative city. Mother wanted to look for a bride for me as she felt that at twenty-six it was time for me to get married. I dismissed the notion as nonsensical, and she was getting very frustrated.

My parents, my older brother Paapu, his wife Shanthi and I lived in a joint family. In December 1973, Shanthi's uncle and aunt, and their daughter, Latha, came to Madras to visit her. Latha's father, Ramaswamy, was in the army, from where he later retired as a colonel. Shanthi and Latha were very fond of each other. Latha had missed Shanthi's wedding because of her college exams. Their family was now visiting us during her vacation. Mother was immediately very taken with Latha when they came home for dinner.

I was at work in the Mill then, and would return home only after 10 p.m., as usual. That evening, though, Mother telephoned, telling me to come home early for dinner. She had never done that before but wouldn't tell me the reason when I asked her.

It became clear enough when I came home and saw Latha with Shanthi and a twinkle in Mother's eyes. I knew there was something afoot. We spent about an hour together; I started arguing about something and Latha argued back. After the visitors went home, my sister-in-law and my mother kept asking me in turns: 'How do you like the girl? Do you like the girl?' So I said, 'Yes, I like her.'

The next day Mother sent word through Shanthi that she would like Latha as a bride for me. Latha is a strong-willed person and her first query was, 'Did Jaggu say this or your mother-in-law? If it's your mother-in-law, I'm not interested.' Shanti suggested that we meet and find out more about each other.

Latha was studying to be a doctor at the Armed Forces Medical College in Pune. She meant to work after her studies and wanted an assurance from me that I would not object to it. I had no objection at all, and that settled the matter. Latha is two years younger than me; she was twenty-four when we got married in 1974. The wedding was a seven-day event, and it seemed like all of Madras was there.

Being an army family, the Ramaswamys had lived in various parts of the country and were far removed from the world of business and its hierarchies in Madras. But with my mother's affectionate guidance, Latha fit into the family with ease.

As it transpired, she did not work as a doctor as we moved to Bangalore (now Bengaluru) soon afterwards and started a family of our own. But I had told Latha to acquire whatever qualification was needed to practise in the US. Until 1984, going back to the US was always an option for me. We never moved from Bangalore, of course.

In later years, Latha's additional medical qualifications in tissue matching and typing at Hoxworth Blood Center, University of Cincinnati, Ohio, were put to great use at the Rotary TTK Blood Bank, under the aegis of the Bangalore Medical Services Trust (BMST), which is one of the largest blood transfusion centres and blood component facilities in Karnataka.

3B

AN ANCHOR AND A GUIDE

*In business, one should not only look at the big picture
but also have an eye for detail.*

My mother, Padma Narasimhan, was a rare human being and greatly influenced me. She was my anchor throughout my life, urging me to aim for a gold medal at IIT, firming up my confidence when I was ill and standing strong beside me through all the storms in our business.

During my third year at IIT, I developed a health problem. White spots appeared all over my body; they appeared out of the blue and spread quickly. I went through a sort of depression. My parents took me that winter to London to get treated. But the doctors said they had never seen such a case before and could not cure me.

I rejoined the campus for the fourth year. It was the toughest year for me because I was depressed that the white spots remained. It was hard to endure the condition. My mother was a great support throughout that period. She used to say

this: 'If you are not conscious of it, nobody else will notice it.'
Her continuous reassurance boosted my confidence and I stood
first in my batch that year.

One of the well-known quiz masters of the time used to
quote a limerick that gave me a lot of confidence and helped me
ignore my condition:

> As a beauty I am not a star,
> There are others more handsome, by far;
> But my face, I don't mind it,
> Because I'm behind it;
> It's the folks out in front that I jar.

Later, when I went to Cornell to study, I sought treatment at
the Massachusetts General Hospital in Boston. I was treated by
the world's most famous dermatologist at the time, Dr Thomas
B. Fitzpatrick. My case was published in the *Harvard Medical
Journal* and my condition came to be known as the 'Fitzpatrick
syndrome'. He treated me free of charge, but there was no cure
for my condition. I was allergic to the usual skin creams, so they
were of no help and I had to live with that. It was not contagious
or infectious, it was just a pigment problem.

The white patches faded away over the next twenty years.
Nobody knows why they came or how they went; it's a medical
mystery.

The hand that rocks

Amma was just thirteen and a half years old when she married
Father. She became the lynchpin of the joint family. She was very

active in social work, and while she was aware of the business deals of the Group, she had not taken an active interest in it.

I don't think it had ever occurred to Father to seek her help, even when he started to tire of keeping the floundering companies going. When he asked me to move to Bangalore, I realized someone had to take over the reins in Madras.

One of the mistakes that Father had made was in his choice of employees, and this cost the company heavily. Many of them were not committed to the business but had over the years become entrenched in the system.

While I could get the business to start earning revenues again, I needed someone to hold the fort to ensure that the revenues were not frittered or siphoned away. I turned to Mother out of desperation, because there really was no one else at that point to whom I could turn.

She was in her forties when I asked her to help out in the business, and she displayed an eye for detail that proved to be a great asset. I didn't consult Father about involving Mother, as from the very day that he handed over the running of the business to me, he had stopped asking me questions or taking any decisions related to the business. He trusted my ability to make the right decisions.

I put the facts in front of her and told her that if she didn't step in we would be finished. I played back to her the same story that she and Father had given me when they got me back from Cornell: Father and Paapu were not in a position to do anything to help, and Raghu was too young. So it was up to the two of us to handle things.

She realized that her involvement was vital and started coming to the office in 1974. Her job description was to 'control the bandicoots and bring down the losses'.

Mother's eye for detail

Mother watched the employees in Madras to determine if they were merely inefficient or were deliberately harming the business. Distressingly, we discovered that many of the senior executives had misused Father's trust. They had got him to sign promissory notes to borrow at very high interest rates, and continued to do so. They were not running the businesses efficiently or profitably either.

But we couldn't sack all the suspect employees en masse; their subterfuge had to be ascertained carefully, and it took a long time to clean the stables. Mother had an impressive technique of dealing with them; she would summon the person in question to her office, look him in the eye, point to the issue that affected the company, and ask, 'Please explain this to me because I am not a businesswoman.' Her straightforward questions helped sift out the bad eggs, and many such employees left the company after realizing their game was up.

To be frank, I did not expect my mother to accomplish what she did, and I was quite impressed with the splendid job she did. Her attention to detail was phenomenal, and this is true of most women. Men tend to look at the big picture, but the devil is in the detail. From 1977 to 2000, until she developed Parkinson's, Mother came to the office every day.

My great regret is that I was not able to clear all the loans that the Group had accumulated while she was alive. We had whittled away the mountain of debts, which at its peak amounted to about Rs 14 crore. The last chunk of debt was Rs 25 lakh. My mission was completed three months after Padma Narasimhan, my mother, my rock, passed away; she did not live long enough to see the debts repaid in full in December 2002.

She died at the age of seventy-three, on 11 September, the anniversary of 9/11. I was in Brussels and could not make it back in time for her funeral. As per our custom, she was cremated the same day; my elder brother had died in 1979, so my younger brother performed the last rites. Her death was a devastating blow to me.

Dignity personified

Latha Jagannathan says this about her mother-in-law: 'Both my father-in-law and mother-in-law were great people, and I too had wanted to live with them in a joint family, like my cousin, Shanthi. But Jaggu had to take over Prestige in Bangalore, and we had to move. My father-in-law was a visionary, but when my mother-in-law joined the business, she was a big help because she looked into the details; that was her strength.

'My mother-in-law was very impressive; she dressed elegantly and spoke very well. She had a great way, a quiet but firm dignity, with which she dealt with the employees who were not performing. She was a very strong personality, and her values were based on the Hindu philosophy of duty. For her, things were black and white, good or bad.

'Like Jaggu, she hated to lose at anything, and our sons are the same. They are all very competitive, whether we played Trivial Pursuit or any other game. The competitive trait that Jaggu inherited from his mother, though, helped him in the business.'

Ajay Thakore, who has first-hand knowledge of the evolution of the TTK Group, recalls, 'Padma Narasimhan was part of every major decision taken by the family regarding the business. She maintained a delicate balance between the older employees, who were very cautious, and the young and energetic Jagannathan, who wanted to change things in a hurry. She handled this task with great tact and good instincts.'

Nauzer Nowroji, former marketing director of TTK Group and TTK Prestige, says, 'Padma Narasimhan was a fascinating person. She would discuss the *rahu kalam* (the auspicious–inauspicious times set in the Hindu calendar) before every product launch. She would come before the event started, speak encouraging words to the whole team and say a prayer. Though her visits were not for longer than fifteen minutes, they were very special, and we looked forward to her words as a benediction.'

4

A PRESSURE COOKER EXPERIENCE

Failure is never an option; you face the challenge, and persevere.

Latha and I didn't go on our honeymoon immediately after our wedding in 1974. As I was an avid race-goer, I had taken Latha to Bangalore instead, for I hadn't wanted to miss the horse-racing season there. She still hasn't forgiven me for this. Sometime later, we took off to the US for a belated honeymoon. While there, we received a telegram from Father asking us to return to Madras immediately.

He received us at the airport and handed me an envelope with a plane ticket, and said, 'I need you to go to Bangalore tomorrow, to run TT Ltd [which was the name of TTK Prestige then].' I had by then come to expect sudden instructions from the family, having been hauled back once from Cornell University to Madras. And now in 1975, yet again, I dutifully left to take up my new assignment.

I had as little knowledge of pressure cookers as I had about any of the other Group businesses. But, having turned around

Maps and Atlases, my confidence was high, and I was game to try my hand at yet another challenge.

I was totally unprepared for the complications that were in store. At the time Father had asked me to move to Bangalore, it didn't seem to be a hardship. I had visited the city often as a child, and we used to stay in the Group's guest house on enjoyable winter vacations. Apart from its weather, I enjoyed the anonymity this city offered, unlike the high-profile existence that our family members had to lead in Madras. People here did not interfere in the personal lives of others, and I liked this facet of Bangalore. After I moved here, I refused to return to Madras, and here I have stayed.

Branching out in Bangalore

The first factory that the TTK Group had set up in Bangalore was Right Aids Orient (P) Ltd, in 1951. This unit manufactured pens and inks under the Waterman brand.

The Group chose to put up the factory in Bangalore because Madras State (present-day Tamil Nadu) during those years did not have enough electricity for industries. The neighbouring state of Mysore (present-day Karnataka), which had legacy of engineering and industry from the pre-Independence era, was able to provide the required power, and Chief Minister Kengal Hanumanthaiah invited industries to establish their manufacturing units in the state.

After cheaper Indian pens and inks diminished the market for Waterman products, in 1955, the plant began to manufacture a variety of Pond's cosmetic and skincare products. TTK & Co. had initially sought to set up a joint venture for this in Madras, but Chief Minister Rajagopalachari turned it down on the grounds that 'Sita [the wife of Rama in the Ramayana] did not use cosmetics and I don't see why Indian women need it now'.

True to his principle of not helping the business he had founded, my grandfather, T.T. Krishnamachari, who was then the Union industries minister, had refused to get involved. The government, however, approved a proposal by Pond's, USA, to set up a factory, and TTK & Co. started contract-manufacturing Pond's Dreamflower talc, vanishing cream, cold cream and a range of Vaseline products in Bangalore. When the Pond's business grew, the factory was moved to Madras in 1961.

Another new venture named TT Private Ltd also operated from the same premises. This was a dairy engineering company that collaborated with firms from Denmark, Holland and Germany to erect dairy plants in India. It also manufactured components for dairy plants and other engineering industries.

Prestige comes to India

Father had started importing pressure cookers from Prestige UK in the early fifties. They were very well received by the Indian consumers, and sensing a bigger opportunity, Father approached Prestige with an offer to collaborate. A collaboration agreement between Prestige and TTK was signed in 1955 to manufacture Prestige cookers in India. In a rather curiously worded order, the government of India permitted the agreement under the condition that a minimum of 2000 cookers be manufactured each month.

Machines were imported from the UK, along with the requisite transfer of technology and training. Installing the

250-tonne press posed a huge challenge, and a crane had to be brought all the way from Calcutta for this. It also involved the cooperation of the Electricity Board and the Highways Authority, apart from several hundred people, to erect it. In 1959, the first of Prestige's Made in India aluminium pressure cookers were produced in the factory.

Today the pressure cooker is an indispensable apparatus in every Indian kitchen, be it humble or luxe. India makes 15 million pressure cookers each year, and TTK Prestige accounts for a staggering 5 million of them. Prestige is by far the market leader, outpacing the closest contender (Hawkins) by a cool million, with the rest of the numbers being made up by small manufacturers, who are mostly in the unorganized sector.

Every third pressure cooker sold in the country bears the TTK Prestige label. They come in various shapes and colours, in aluminium, stainless steel, hard anodized and plastic (microwaveable), and are churned out from Prestige's five state-of-the-art factories located in east, west, central and south India.

The pressure cooker market is one that is constantly in traction. Apart from first-time homemakers buying new cookers, customers are hooked to the 'exchange' offers that lure them to replace their old models with newer ones that have more exciting features.

Cookers make up only 35 per cent of the TTK Prestige business, as the company went on to extend its scope, offering over 600 appliances for the kitchen and home. It wouldn't be an exaggeration to say that every Indian home surely has at least one Prestige product. Undoubtedly, pressure cookers are the foundation of Prestige's success.

A rocky start

My initiation into our Prestige business was quite a pressure cooker experience for me, starting from the very first day.

The factory was located in Doorvaninagar, which was then in the outskirts of Bangalore. It had been in business for fifteen years and had been yielding decent profits. When the managing director, C.V. Chandrashekhar, had to be replaced, my father sent me to take over the reins. That was easier said than done, as I was very soon to realize.

On the crisp winter morning of 1 January 1975, I made my way to the factory, full of vim and vigour, only to receive a very rude shock. When I reached the gates, the security guards would not let me enter the factory. The previous managing director had steadily fostered suspicion and hostility against my family, and the disgruntled employees didn't want me as their boss.

In all honesty, I couldn't blame the employees for their ill-will. While all the other businesses of the TTK Group located in Madras were floundering, the pressure cooker business based in Bangalore had been doing well. The employees felt the profits they helped generate were being used to prop up the ailing businesses back in Madras, and they resented it. The employees felt that I would not act in the best interests of TT Limited (as the Prestige business was then known) and, at the behest of the previous MD, stopped me from entering the factory.

Workers' ire

I had to seek the intervention of the police to gain entry into the factory. It was not the most propitious beginning, and, as I soon learnt, getting into the factory was just the first hurdle. The employees made it very clear that they didn't want me occupying the managing director's seat.

It is not a challenge that a twenty-six-year-old starting in business usually faces, but face it I had to, and with only myself to rely upon. I couldn't ask my father to come down and admonish the people who wouldn't acknowledge me as their boss.

I decided then to prove myself to the employees there. Respecting their wishes, I didn't occupy the managing director's seat. Instead, I hauled another small desk into the office and started working from there.

No one entered the office or spoke to me for a whole month. I had brought with me an executive assistant from Madras. He used to sit in the staff room and would hear people talking about me. They thought I would destroy the company and close it down. The biggest challenge in front of me was to change their mindset and overcome their hostility.

Failure was not an option. I needed the staff and the workers to operate the machines and keep the production going. For example, if I wanted to change a process I had to tell the chief engineer to implement it. I couldn't go to the factory floor and start changing things myself. I realized that I had to win my people over, lest my entry into the factory became a pyrrhic victory.

The employees watched with great interest as I continued to work sitting at the small desk. No doubt they were surprised that I respected their resentment at my appointment.

Proving my mettle

The change was very slow to come, but it happened when the factory experienced a problem that led to stoppage of production. Aluminium was the critical metal that we needed to make pressure cookers, and its supply had come to an abrupt stop, leaving the machines and men idle.

The Indian aluminium industry was controlled by the government for about eighteen years, from 1970 till March 1989. Both the price and distribution of aluminium were regulated, though rather informally, until 1975. Distribution rules became stringent in July 1975 when it was brought under the purview of the Aluminium Control Order.

Curbs were imposed on aluminium producers; they now had to produce 50 per cent of their metal as EC (electrical conductor) grade in the shape of ingots and wire rods. These would have to be supplied to units against allotments made by the Aluminium Controller (yes, there was such a post in those days).

My predecessor had erred in the representation that our company had made to the government, and TTK Prestige was allotted a very small quota of the metal. Without raw material, what could the factory produce? The machines stood still, and there was much anxiety among the 400 employees. It was then that the staff approached me, asking for a solution.

We had to rectify the company's earlier submission, and I went to Delhi to seek an allotment of aluminium for the company. It was three months before I was able to meet the Aluminium Controller and present him with our request. Those were the days of the Licence Raj, and navigating the corridors of power was an intimidating task. The factory was closed for four months until my revised representation was accepted. This got us 35 tonnes of aluminium a month (Today, we use up 700 tonnes a month). The quota would allow us to supply only in south India, but it was enough for us to restart production.

Earning trust

This also gained me a small measure of trust among the factory staff and workers, but if I had hoped that they would embrace me with enthusiasm, I was mistaken. That was still a long way off. They would not let me interfere with the design or manufacture. 'This has come from UK, we can't change anything,' was their adamant stance.

They wouldn't listen to me and I couldn't sack any of them—who would run the company if I did so? Their attitude said, 'You might be the chairman's son, but we know more about this business than you do.'

And they were right. I knew nothing. True, I was an engineer, a gold medallist from IIT Madras with a master's degree in operations research from Cornell. But I had never used a pressure cooker in my life. I didn't even know how to operate it and, truth to tell, I was scared of pressure cookers.

I did the only obvious thing I could do and worked on earning the respect and trust of the employees, demonstrating my interest in the company and working hard alongside them. It took me two years to earn their trust, at the end of which the employees themselves came to me and requested me to sit on the chair designated for the managing director.

Magical device

Pressure cookers brought a bit of magic into the Indian kitchen. It's no wonder that they took the local market by storm when they were launched and have gone on to make the fortunes of many a domestic manufacturing company and retailer.

Traditionally, rice, dal, vegetables and meat used to be cooked separately. It was a long-drawn-out process, taking up to two hours, and also needed constant attendance, as the pots had to be watched and their contents stirred from time to time. Food cooks faster in a pressure cooker than in conventional pots. Pressure is created by boiling water or any other liquid inside a closed container. Steam builds up and is trapped inside, increasing the pressure and, consequently, the temperature within the container. This allows the food to cook in just twenty minutes. The pressure is then gradually reduced, allowing the lid of the cooker to be opened safely. The cooking process happens without the gadget having to be constantly minded; pressure cooking enables many kinds of food to be cooked in just a single vessel and on a single stove, and also saves energy.

The magic of the pressure cooker had to be demonstrated, and in the days before apartment complexes, the best way to reach many women was through the AWWA (Army Wives' Welfare Association). Prestige held many demonstration sessions under the aegis of AWWA to popularize the pressure cooker.

History of pressure cookers

The first pressure cooker was perhaps demonstrated in May 1689, when Denis Papin, a French physicist, exhibited his invention, 'steam digester', to the Royal Society in London. The steam digester was used to cook bones. It was not until 1915 that the term 'pressure cooker' was first used, and mention of this term was first made in the *Journal of Home Economics*.

The first commercially manufactured pressure cooker was introduced at the New York World's Fair in 1939, and National Presto Company introduced the aluminium Presto pressure cookers in the USA in 1953.

The technology came to India in 1959. While H.D. Vasudeva started to manufacture Hawkins cookers in India in collaboration with L.G. Hawkins of England, the TTK Group started making Prestige pressure cookers in India in collaboration with Prestige UK.[1]

---

[1]   Source: www.indiacurry.com

5

THE INVENTION THAT
SAVED PRESTIGE

*If you want to know the truth about your product,
go to the market and meet your dealers/customers.*

'Your cookers are bursting, and nobody wants to buy them.'
With these words, a shopkeeper in Lucknow flung open the
doors of his warehouse to show me row upon row of pressure
cookers, all of them bearing the Prestige brand, all of which had
exploded.

I simply couldn't believe my eyes. We had never experienced
anything like this, and I could swear by all that I held dear about
the quality of our production. How, then, had these cookers
burst?

After taking up the reins at Prestige in 1975, I had won over
the hostile employees and solved the shortage of aluminium that
had crippled production. We got a small quota of aluminium,
and that allowed us to make enough cookers to supply south
India only.

By 1978 the shortage of aluminium had started to ease, and we were back to supplying our customers India-wide. But while the sales of our cookers picked up in the south, they were not doing well in the north, and I set out to find out why.

Market visits

While travelling the length and breadth of Uttar Pradesh, I discovered to my shock that our pressure cookers were bursting. I met with dealers and visited warehouses where I saw the defective pressure cookers, and they were all Prestige cookers. Small wonder then that our cookers were not selling.

Nobody had told me about the problem, and though what I found was disturbing, I was glad that I had gone to the market to see it for myself. And that is a learning that I have always remembered.[1] I made it a point to frequently visit most of our dealers, and so did my senior team members. You can never get the right information, especially the bad news, from third parties.

I realized that if we didn't stop this from happening we wouldn't have a business to run. A bursting cooker can kill a person; it was not surprising that nobody was buying our cookers. That night I stayed up late in my hotel room and tried to figure out how to fix the problem.

My engineering knowledge came to my aid, and I figured out that the cookers were bursting because of spurious spare parts. While we sold good safety plugs along with the cooker, the life

---

[1]   T.T. Raghunathan, executive chairman of TTK Healthcare, says about his brother, 'My brother is a legend in the cookware space. He knows every dealer. Even in ill health he goes to the market.'

cycle of a pressure cooker is longer than that of its external parts; a cooker can last up to fifty years.

Spurious parts

Customers were unknowingly buying spurious spare safety plugs. The safety plugs are made of tin bismuth, an expensive alloy. Cheaper plugs were an attractive alternative for ignorant customers.

That is the grim reality in India—spurious drugs, food and spare parts are sold aplenty. The dealers don't worry about what they sell, so long as it sells. Since it wasn't possible for me to single-handedly stop the use of such spares, I had to come up with a solution that would prevent the cookers from bursting even if inferior-quality parts were used.

I called the chief engineer at our factory and instructed him to keep a mock-up ready for me to work on. When I returned to Bangalore and hastened to the factory I found that the engineer had not followed my instructions. His stand was that if what I had suggested had been possible, 'the people in Prestige UK would have done it. If they couldn't do it, how could we do it?'

His thinking was not very different from that of most Indians in those days; witness the Ambassador car that India manufactured under licence from a British firm for fifty years without a single change. That was the obdurate mindset of the times.

Inventing the GRS

I worked in the lab for a whole month and came up with the Gasket Release System, or GRS, my first innovation. A pressure cooker comes with a weight valve that is meant to rise up and release the steam that is built up by the pressure inside the cooker. The valve then settles back in place. The safety plug is a back-up safety mechanism and regulates the pressure built up in the cooker if the weight valve fails. Spurious safety plugs that were being sold for Prestige pressure cookers did not work effectively, and instead of regulating the pressure and releasing steam, they led to the cookers exploding.

The gasket is the rubber ring that is inserted within the outer rim of the pressure cooker, and its task is to hold the lid firmly in place even as the pressure builds up inside the cooker.

The Gasket Release System is an effective safety device. It ensures that if the weight valve or the safety plug fails to function, either because the cooker is overloaded or the vent is blocked, a portion of the gasket is pushed out through a slot in the lid, thus releasing the excess steam down and away from the person at the kitchen counter. The GRS is equally effective even if spurious spares are used.

I can confidently claim that not a single Prestige pressure cooker has burst since that day. The GRS is just a hole in the lid. But if it were not for that hole, the company would have gone bankrupt.

Over the course of time, other manufacturers too have been using the GRS in their cookers. We welcomed it. I did not patent the GRS for a very strategic reason. Pressure cookers had by then become synonymous with Prestige, and even when a cooker made by another manufacturer burst, the newspapers reported it as a Prestige pressure cooker. I wanted to ensure that our brand would not be affected, and by allowing other manufacturers to use the GRS, we could improve the safety of all pressure cookers and serve the interests of the consumers.

Communicating with customers

Now that we had made pressure cookers safe, I wanted to proclaim our safety innovation in the media. The advertising agency that had been working with us until then didn't see eye to eye with me about doing a huge media campaign.

One evening I met my good friend Bunty Peerbhoy, who owned MAA Communications, and asked him to take up the advertising campaign. His wife, Sadiqa, came up with the iconic line for the ad film: '*Jo biwi se karey pyaar, woh Prestige se karey kaise inkaar?*' This line continues to be paraphrased in many ways by people across India.

Since millions of non-GRS pressure cookers were already out in the market, we began removing them. We ran service camps city by city, checking the cookers brought in by our customers. We ran the cookers through hardness meters to examine whether they were safe. If the cookers were safe, we would educate the customers about the importance of buying original spares and also give them a list of shops where they could buy authentic spares. Whenever we found an unsafe cooker we offered to exchange it for a new one at an attractively discounted price.

Some customers were unwilling to part with their old cookers, perhaps out of the sentimental value it held for them. In such cases we cautioned them to use the vessel only for steaming, if they still wanted to use the gadget, but not its pressure facility.

The camps became a great channel of communication, and we ran them for close to fifteen years to make sure customers were educated about the proper use of the pressure cooker and the importance of using genuine spares. Even though we advertised the safety features in the mass media, we found that one-on-one interactions were very important and effective.

A service camp would typically run for fourteen to fifteen hours a day. Our staff would meet customers till nine in the evening, explaining in simple and clear terms the whole process, apart from carrying out a complete check of their pressure cookers. This is the way we ensured our brand retained the loyalty of its customers.

The GRS also reinforced the respect with which my colleagues regarded me. From being extremely hostile to tolerant, they began to display, dare I say, some admiration?

A series of innovations in product design and service, coupled with the buying of the Prestige brand, set us on a steady course from 1975 to 1994. We also realized a crucial truth—that we needed to be in direct contact with the dealers and communicate with customers.

Innovating the pressure pan

Working in the lab on the GRS had me hankering to tinker around more, and I set up a product development department, with myself as the sole staffer.

The first product that came out from this department was the pressure pan. I felt this product was highly suitable for India as Indian cooking involves a lot of frying of the food before its cooking. A pressure pan would suit all the requirements, replacing the use of multiple kadais and cookers.

I must admit that, again, the chief engineer was sceptical as we hadn't received this wisdom from England. This is another instance of the resistance to change that I encountered in doing business. But we went ahead and launched the Prestige Pressure Pan to great success.

Nauzer Nowroji calls the pressure pan a 'breakthrough' product of the nineties:

It was the first innovative product by Prestige made locally for the Indian market, and it was a runaway success. We had noticed that people tended to garnish the food in the cooker vessel. That led to R&D and a well-developed local product that even Prestige UK didn't have. This gave us a huge marketing boost as it was innovative, had clearly positioned itself and subsequently led to our selling a common lid for two vessels—the cooker and the pan. The combined packaging was again successful in driving up sales. The pressure pan also allowed us to penetrate the north Indian market as Hawkins didn't have such a feature. (Hawkins Cookers Ltd has not launched a pressure pan to date.)[2]

Buying the Prestige brand

I was sure that this was the first of market-changing innovations from us, and it did act as a catalyst for us to gain ownership of the brand. It was a momentous decision, not just for our Prestige business but for the Group too, as all the businesses under the TTK Group were selling Western brands under licence.

Until this time we were using the Prestige brand under licence, and there was always the possibility that it could be taken away

---

[2]   Source: www.hawkinscookers.com

from us at any time. Apart from the financial outlay, we were now making significant investments in technology, and I could not live with the fear that we could lose the brand. The only sure way to ensure that the brand stayed with us was to buy it.

I went to England, and after very difficult negotiations bought the Prestige brand for India in 1992. It gave me great satisfaction to own the brand that we were working so hard to popularize, even though we owned the name only in India. This was also the first time that we had owned a brand. It was a wonderful feeling.

Going for steel

With the Prestige brand wholly ours in India, we diversified into steel cookers. Hitherto our pressure cookers were made only of aluminium, and between 1990 and 1994, we launched stainless steel cookers and non-stick cookware under a technical tie-up with Dupont, USA.

If you were to ask me why some people buy aluminium cookers and some buy stainless steel, I would say they are personal preferences. Some people like stainless steel and some prefer aluminium. The preference varies across regions. In Europe the preference is for steel pressure cookers. Except for England and Greece, not a single aluminium cooker is sold in the rest of the European Union. Japan too prefers stainless steel cookers. In the US, there are higher sales of aluminium cookers because the Hispanic population favours them.

Stainless steel lasts longer and retains its appearance better in the long term (though now we have a range of very attractive hard-anodized cookers and cookware). Aluminium is actually more efficient because it is a better conductor of heat and cooks food faster. There is a fear that has been created that aluminium is bad for the health, but it is completely false. An antacid pill is made up of aluminium hydroxide. A person suffering from acidity consumes the equivalent of one pressure cooker in two years, and it hasn't harmed anyone.

The price difference between aluminium and stainless steel cookers is quite significant, as a steel cooker costs twice as much as an aluminium cooker.

Yet another unfounded fear is that non-stick cookware, which need less oil to cook and are easier to clean, is bad for the health. There are studies showing that polytetrafluoroethylene (PTFE)—the non-stick material that is used to coat the pans— is completely inert. The vessels have to be used properly, though. They are best used on low or medium heat. You can heat a non-stick pan up to 260°C (500°F) without damaging the finish. This is well above the temperatures required for boiling and frying. Empty pans should not be pre-heated as they can reach high temperatures in minutes and the food may burn. Non-stick vessels should be replaced after five years, and earlier if they are chipped.

All our products aim to enhance the lives of people. My parents would never have countenanced an unsafe or unhealthy product or service. That is why we don't make liquor or cigarettes. We don't make anything that is known to be detrimental to the health of the people.

IPO: A tough decision

In 1993 we decided to make TT Prestige a public company. It was a major readjustment, to switch from being a family-held company to a listed entity. We had gone through similar changes when we had listed TTK Healthcare in 1985. The issue was oversubscribed fifty-three times, a record back then.

It had not been an easy decision for either company, and I think going public can never be an easy decision for a family-run company. While the IPO gets the company money from the public, it also gives any shareholder the right to question our decisions and actions. We have to justify everything we want to do. It took a lot of persuasion by Ajay Thakore and the others to convince Mother and me to go ahead with taking our companies public. Before we went public, I might have said, 'Let's go buy X company.' But in a listed company, I have to justify the decision, take it to the board, answer their questions and so on. But I feel going public has been worth that adjustment.

In September 1994 we took TT Prestige public at a share price of Rs 90. The issue was oversubscribed thirteen times. We didn't need the money from the IPO to pay off debts, but our reasons were more strategic. As a private company, we were not in the news, whereas our competitor, Hawkins, was a listed company and was in the news all the time. More importantly, a private company does not get valuations. If we had not been a listed company, we would have been worth far less than we are now. While the capital reserves of the company amount to Rs 840 crore ($132.5 million), our market capital is over Rs 8000 crore ($1.26 billion).

Even today, I attend analysts' conferences, where I am asked why I am there as I don't need the money. I tell them that I am there so that they can make money. Unless I popularize the company, my shareholders don't make money.

When we were discussing the pricing of the shares, Shankaran, group director (corporate affairs) at TTK, wanted to peg the issue price at Rs 90 per share, but I felt this was too high and wanted him to bring it down to Rs 60. Shankaran said he had studied the market and knew where the company was going. He said we hadn't realized the brand's intrinsic value. We also needed to cut down on our borrowings from banks, as the interest rate was then 27 per cent.

Adventures galore

The Rs 30 crore we were seeking to raise was a big sum at that time. The western state of Gujarat is key to the stock market; two days before the issue opened, there was an outbreak of plague in Surat, one of the state's important trading cities, and the entire market in the state was closed for two days.

There had already been some drama in the run-up to the IPO. Banks had gone on strike a few days before our launch. Apart from the managers, the rest of the bank staff had struck work.

Those days, posters used to be put up to get word out about forthcoming public offerings, and banks were good places to get the attention of investors. Shankaran and other staff of our company, who were in Bombay for the issue, went to the banks and put up posters themselves.

I was expectedly nervous and repeatedly turned to Shankaran with queries about the fate of our public offering. He reassured me that all we needed was for the issue to be fully subscribed, though he seemed confident that we would be oversubscribed at least a dozen times. I took a vow that I would go to Tirupati and offer my hair, in the ritual of tonsure, to the Lord, if the issue was fully subscribed. It was oversubscribed thirteen times and I kept my vow. Those days I visited Tirupati at least once every few months. My friends often came with me. We travelled in a special van I had that my friends had nicknamed 'Jagmobile'. It was a Standard 20 with a custom-built cards table, and we played cards all through the journey.

With the money that we raised from the IPO, we grew at a comfortable pace of between 8 per cent and 9 per cent, from 1994 to 2000. We launched stainless steel cookers and non-stick cookware, but it was nothing extraordinary. Everything seemed quite mundane and it was a period of boredom for me. If it was excitement that I wanted, I didn't have to wait long as the government was getting ready to serve up a very large dollop of frenzy.

6

DISRUPTING THE OLD ORDER

Change the way you do business; the old ways
won't continue to work.

At its peak, the Group's debt was around Rs 14 crore, and it loomed large in front of us. Father was very clear that we would not default or shirk from our responsibilities, unlike many high-profile businessmen who have done so in recent years.

Prestige was the sole company that was making profits. I applied myself to its growth and ploughed the profits from its steady growth in Bangalore to gradually pay off all the debts run up by the eighteen businesses of the Group back in Madras. I was able to fulfil Father's wish of paying back the loans. Hard work and luck helped free us from debt.

If you ask me to put a finger on what exactly I did to turn the Group around, it consisted of a series of very logical and simple steps.

First, we stopped the losses in the businesses in Madras by gradually weeding out inefficient workers and putting an end to practices such as the signing of promissory notes at high interest rates. With my mother and her eagle-eyed vigilance, we were able to plug the holes, though it took relentless efforts from 1974 to 1990 to do so.

Next, over a period of time, we also bought out my uncles' shares in the business. Grandfather had four sons, and had given over three-fourths of the business to his eldest son, my father, and the rest to two sons—T.T. Rangaswami and T.T. Vasu. Another son, T.T. Raghavan, was in the army, and Grandfather had settled on him property and money instead of shares in the family business. The settlement with my uncles did cause some heartburn, but we gave them a very fair financial deal even though the business was making losses.

Depositors' trust

The heartening aspect of our journey was the trust the common man vested in us. While we owed money to many lenders and to a few banks, a lot of deposits had come from people who had invested their pensions and Provident Fund money with us. Father didn't want to let them down, and that was the major reason he wanted the Group to engineer a turnaround. The individual depositors had complete faith in Father; they believed he would not let them down. Their trust was the reason for my return.

When we were able to start repaying the loans, we found that these individuals did not want their deposits back; they wanted to continue getting the interest the Group had been paying them. For ten years they had been paid interest of around 15 per cent; no bank was paying more than 8 per cent. Not surprisingly, the depositors wanted to earn the higher interest that we were paying them.

We returned most of the deposits and retained the money of those depositors who were adamant about staying on. We didn't need their deposits any more, but we honoured their request. They had deposited their money with us when we wanted it, so it was not fair that we give it back when we didn't want it. Over the years we have gradually reduced such investments to about Rs 1 crore, a fraction of the Group's market capital of Rs 10,000 crore ($1.57 billion).

Banking woes

Some would argue that banks are a different kettle of fish from individual depositors, and that they can waive or write off loans. Father would not allow that; he insisted that we pay back everything with interest. It is a matter of pride for us that we have never restructured a loan with a bank loan. These were my father's principles, and I abide by them.

By the time Father died in April 2000, we had cleared a substantial chunk of our debts. We didn't negotiate a single loan, though the banks knew that we were going bankrupt. I have never been inside a bank. Even in the days when we were up shit creek, I never went to a bank.

Many banks woo us now; the chairmen of these banks come to my office seeking our business. But there is one bank with which I will not do business. After steadily working our way through our debt situation, paying off close to Rs 14 crore, the last debt that was left was of Rs 25 lakh, which was a lot of money in those days. This sum included Rs 10 lakh in penal interest. But the bank would not waive a penny of that, and we paid them the entire Rs 25 lakh in December 2002.

That was the last time that I did business with that particular bank. We have since taken loans on many occasions and paid them off. But as a matter of principle I don't do business with that bank. A bank should keep its clients happy; if its client is doing well, the bank will do well too.

I felt a huge sense of relief after repaying the loans; 'It's done,' I told myself! I didn't celebrate as Mother had passed away in September, and it weighed heavily on me that I had not been able to clear all of our loans while she was still alive.

On a lighter note, it also meant that I could buy a fancy car, a Mercedes Benz, and drink Scotch like my peers. I had seen money being squandered on luxuries and expensive toys, and that had me resolve that I would not buy a foreign car or drink Scotch whisky (both considered very prestigious in India) until the day we paid off all our debts.

I stuck to this resolve, though friends repeatedly told me that the managing director of Prestige ought to be driving the best car and drinking the best whisky. Even today, I drink only Black & White. And my friends tell me, 'You are one of the richest people in the country. You should not be drinking this, you should be drinking only single malts.' But a leopard can't change its spots. I am very careful with money; in the last sixteen years, I have changed my car only four times.

A man who abhors excess

Bunty Peerbhoy, chairman, MAA, recalls, 'Several decades ago, Jaggu and I had gone for a holiday to Delhi, Agra and a few other places with some friends and our families. Some of the other friends did not want to spend on air tickets so Jaggu booked all of us into third-class train compartments.

'He also booked a very humble place called Yatri Nivas for us to stay in Delhi. I remember vividly that two of his top executives came to meet him while we were there, and Jaggu wasn't the least bit embarrassed to meet them at a place which had broken windows. His executives were staying at the luxurious Taj Mansingh!

'TTJ will not fly first class even today, unless he gets upgraded. Otherwise he flies business class. Earlier, he used to fly economy, and does so even now while on holiday. He says, "When I travel on work, the company pays the business class fare, for it makes money as a result of my travel. But when I go on a holiday, why should I pay more when an economy seat can get me to the same place?"

'He would rather have his shoes mended than buy a new pair. If I present him with an expensive pen, he'll say, "What do I want this pen for? It's not going to do anything that my five-rupee throwaway pen can't do."

'He never fusses about the TTK Group and his status—that's what's amazing about the man. He is not a person who believes that money is a differentiator.'

The socialist burden

Our third step was to work our way through legal and financial tangles. We had hit rock bottom in the 1970s, and it took tremendous and sustained effort over twenty-six years before we were able to stem the losses. During this period of struggle, we had to deal with yet another mammoth problem. This was the maze of taxation laws and the many different complications they caused in each of our companies.

Tax law was an area as unknown to me as running a business. In 1973, Father had invited Ajay Thakore, a tax consultant in Bombay, to join the board of TTK Prestige. I would rank him among the sharpest tax minds in India. While navigating our way through the complexities of Indian laws, Ajay's knowledge and access to experts in the field proved valuable, as did his bold stance on many matters.

There were many daunting and complicated issues that we had to deal with, but we were not about to give up without a fight. We took all the issues to court, fought them and won. If you look at the records, we are the biggest litigants. I travelled frequently to Bombay to confer with the best legal minds. We were determined to know all the legal issues in running a business, first-hand. Over those few years, I think I learnt quite a lot about legal matters, income tax, excise, company and labour laws.

A lonely struggle

It took several years to resolve these issues, and as we worked to clear the huge tax liabilities, I struggled to get the businesses going. Seventy per cent of my time was spent on such matters, and I did not have competent or reliable professionals to delegate the work to. Many professionals didn't want to join private family businesses then, and I had to plough through most of the gruelling work myself.

Our attempts to grow the businesses were shackled by the accumulated debts and, ironically, by the socialist laws that Grandfather had put in place as finance minister, an action that was in complete contrast to his days as an entrepreneur. The anti-capitalist laws made it difficult to do business in India. Back then, income tax was 97 per cent, wealth tax 5 per cent, and sometimes there was expenditure tax too. Incredible as it might sound, taxes could also exceed income, forcing businesses to borrow money to pay tax, without even the benefit of interest on such a loan being tax-deductible. And, despite all this, if the business were to make a profit, a super profit tax would be levied!

T.T. Krishnamachari, my grandfather, and Nehru were responsible for these draconian laws that held back the growth of Indian industry. While they were aimed at curbing accumulation of private wealth, they also reined in entrepreneurs. They also led to the rise of the Licence Raj, during which industrialists could not get permissions to do business without greasing the right palms.

We persevered, and the TTK Group transited into the new economic order that came about with the liberalization of the Indian economy in 1991.

A nose for matters legal

Ajay Thakore, tax consultant and former member of the TTK board, says:

'Jaggu was the junior-most person when he joined the company, and the senior executives at that time were not competent to handle the various complex tax problems that would have cost the company millions.

'I was a relatively junior tax consultant at that time, and on certain very complicated points we had to consult luminaries in Bombay, like Nani Palkhivala and J.C. Shah. Jaggu didn't send his executives to such meetings; he would attend each and every meeting himself, after which we would take a joint decision. This helped us solve the problems faster.

'He is a highly intelligent person, and this gift helped him when he had to go deep into provisions of the Companies Act and had to solve tax issues. In a few years he became an authority on taxation and company law, and all his friends started consulting him, as if he were a tax consultant.

'Family firms like TTK were running on borrowings from outsiders. But then, new laws came in that limited public deposits, and this would affect the Group. Every time I went to Bangalore or Madras, I used to bring up the topic and talk about the example of Dhirubhai Ambani, who had grown Reliance by making it a public company. For quite some time the family was against it, but I convinced them that TTK Prestige should become public. When I look at its growth today, I feel very proud that I know Jaggu.'

Restructuring the Group

A major surgery was needed for the TTK Group companies, and quickly. After we stopped them from bleeding money by 1990, we had to move along the upward slope of the J curve and start making profits, and soon.

We constituted a Group Operating Committee (GOC) to formulate the Group's vision for the future. The GOC began to meet once a quarter for an extended meeting, when, over two and a half days, the head of each company put forth his strategy and new ideas. It brought to light many discrepancies in the thinking and execution as we saw startling contradictions in the different presentations that came to the table.

The contradictions can be traced back to the energetic but uncoordinated growth of the businesses.

Born during colonial rule, the TTK Group was an indenting agency, and pioneered the distribution of consumer goods. In the 1950s it ventured into manufacturing after India became free. Father had set up several companies to manufacture a diverse range of products that included well-known brands such as Woodward's Gripe Water, Prestige cookers and Durex condoms. Some of the manufacturing was through joint ventures while others were under licence. We also began to create our own swadeshi brands such as TTK Tantex.

In the 1980s, the TTK Group was in multiple businesses through various entities. Some of these companies were:

+ TT Private Ltd (manufacturing pressure cookers; now known as TTK Prestige Ltd)
+ Prestige Housewares India Ltd (making barbecues, etc.)

+ TTK Pharma Ltd (making consumer products and pharmaceuticals; later became TTK Healthcare Ltd)
+ TTK Chemicals Ltd (making basic drugs and antibiotics)
+ London Rubber Company of India Ltd (manufacturing condoms and latex examination gloves; became TTK LIG Ltd and then TTK Protective Devices Ltd)
+ Lorcom Protectives Ltd (making condoms first, then gloves, syringes, blood bags, sutures, etc., i.e. medical disposables; later became TTK Biomed Ltd)
+ TT Cardboards Ltd
+ TT Maps and Printers Ltd
+ TT Investments and Trades Ltd (making Tantex branded hosiery and spinning; became TTK Tantex Ltd)
+ Titan Precision Industries Ltd (manufacture of paper cones, i.e. textile intermediary)
+ New Way Chemicals Pvt. Ltd (making Kiwi shoe polish)

Realigning our companies

In 1990, we took a momentous decision that TTK & Co. would give up the business of distribution and hand over the marketing and distribution functions to the respective companies. Until then, all the products made by the various Group companies were distributed by T.T. Krishnamachari & Co., be they cookers, gripe water, condoms, hosiery or anything else.

This decision came about as a result of the GOC and was triggered by the significant insights they had gathered. They brought to light several complexities and problems in the old way of doing business. To start with, the new tax structures made trading among the Group companies questionable.

Brand ownership

We also found that we were spending a lot more than we should have been. TTK & Co. was buying products at cost price from factories and was spending considerable money on marketing brands owned by somebody else. This nudged us into buying the legacy brands of Prestige in 1992 (from Prestige UK) and Woodward's Gripe Water in 1997–98 (this was also a British brand, and the licence was held by the joint venture, TTK–LIG) as we had invested enormously in building these brands and they had become synonymous with TTK in India.

Decentralizing marketing

The most critical realization was that marketing could no longer be a centralized function. TTK & Co. was acting as a distributor, merely selling whatever the manufacturing units produced. On the other hand, our general managers were acting as factory managers, merely producing as per orders received; they worked in isolation and were not connected to matters such as market share.

This had been affecting the progress of the companies, as accountability was not clearly defined and there was no ownership for product innovation and no impetus for growth. The old hierarchy had to change.

It was clear that without a strong hand constantly monitoring and guiding a coordinated course, the businesses would not grow. I decided then that I would not take on this onus as it could not be viable in the long term; instead, the businesses would become responsible for their own growth.

We decided to replace the old order with an integrated process that would put the focus on product, growth and innovation. We dissolved the centralized marketing division and integrated the entire business into verticals that aligned with the manufacturing businesses.

For example, we created TTK Healthcare by merging the pharma and baby-care businesses. Prestige, Maps and Atlases and Tantex also became integrated businesses with their own marketing support. The distribution of Prestige pressure cookers was handed over to TT Private Ltd, the distribution of Tantex hosiery to TT Industries, the distribution of Woodward's Gripe Water and pharmaceuticals to TTK Pharma Ltd, etc. We decided to merge a few businesses; for example, we merged TTK Chemicals into TTK Pharma. We also consolidated the printing and maps business into TTK Pharma to add to its asset base.

In the process, we shed a few businesses that were not strategic—for example, Titan Precision Industries Ltd—and also created new businesses. TTK Biomed formed another JV with Maersk group to focus on manufacturing medical disposables. The new joint venture was called TTK Maersk Medical Ltd. New Way Chemicals became Sara Lee TTK after a JV with the Sara Lee group for manufacturing the Kiwi range and the Brylcreem range; these products were to be distributed by TTK Healthcare.

The reorganization was a very major change, and it transformed the whole business. We created strategy plans for each company, which helped the Group get better focus and build long-term capabilities. Prestige, which was the flagship company of the Group even then, was all set to take a huge leap in growth. Out of all this was also born our vision statement: 'Quality consumer products at affordable prices'. The future looked bright and we set out to conquer the world.

The TTK–Nehru Budget of 1957 and its repercussions

As finance minister in Jawaharlal Nehru's cabinet, TTK was instrumental in creating a protectionist economic policy and pushed for import substitution of consumer goods.

Industries were divided into three categories—Schedule A, consisting of those industries, such as power and heavy manufacturing, which were to be exclusively built by the states; Schedule B, including industries which would be state-owned, but in which private enterprises could supplement the state's efforts, involving industries such as chemicals, transportation and metals; and Schedule C, which included all the industries whose development was left to the private sector.

However, there was a degree of state control here too, through a licensing system. A licence to increase production was issued only if the government was convinced that the country needed the goods.

The 1957 Budget, influenced by the Cambridge post-War economist Kaldor's taxation system, crippled the private sector further. TTK imposed several layers of taxes on the private sector, including expenditure tax, wealth tax, capital tax and gift tax.

These two economic policies set the tone for the country's economy over the next two decades. The share of government investment in large-scale manufacturing industries was increased in comparison to private investment. Industrialization was closely monitored by the state, and several large-scale power projects and steel plants, including the ones in Bhilai, Durgapur and Rourkela, were established during this period. India's imports during that period consisted of raw materials and machinery essential for heavy public-sector industries.

The Indian economic crisis, 1991

While India's imports were going up, exports were declining rapidly due to its closed market system and poor global promotion of its products. This led to a severe balance of payments crisis, which worsened over the years as the country's oil import bill ballooned, triggered by the Gulf War (2 August 1990–28 February 1991).

Credit dried up, and as investors took their money out, the trade deficit led to a severe external payments crisis. The country's forex reserves stood at $1.2 billion, just enough to finance three weeks of essential imports.

To get further credit, India had to pledge 67 tonnes of gold in 1991 to the International Monetary Fund, and this was airlifted out, much to the shock and dismay of the country. That was when Prime Minister P.V. Narasimha Rao and Finance Minister Manmohan Singh introduced the Liberalization, Privatization and Globalization Policy. The rupee was devalued, licensing was abolished, and the Indian market opened to foreign direct investment and foreign products.

At this juncture, India's private industrialists found themselves at a disadvantage against global manufacturers. A closed market and restrictions on foreign investment meant that India's industries were isolated from the many technological developments which had boosted production the world over.

The country had decades of technology to catch up on, and in the meantime, cheaper and better foreign products flooded the domestic market. Indigenous manufacturing was severely hit as traditional manufacturers reeled under the impact of the market changes. The 'Bombay Club', an informal group of leading Indian industrialists, consisting of Lala Bharat Ram, Lalit Mohan Thapar, Hari Shankar Singhania, M.V. Arunachalam, B.K. Modi, C.K. Birla, Rahul Bajaj and Jamshyd Godrej, lobbied the government for protection and a 'level playing field' for Indians. Though the government made some concessions, change could not be stopped, in the larger interests of the country.

Over time, though, it is evident that the economic liberalization also freed Indian businesses from the many shackles that had hitherto hampered their growth. With the Licence Raj consigned to the dust heap, they were free to set their eyes on new horizons, and while quite a few of the traditional businesses lost their sheen, those who quickly learnt the marketplace rules of the new economy have thrived, viz. the Ambanis, Tatas, Birlas.

In parallel, a host of new businesses driven by first-generation entrepreneurs surged in industries that were opened up to the private sector. Some of these entrepreneurs were Sunil Bharti Mittal, in telecommunications; Subhash Chandra, in media and entertainment; and Naresh Goyal, in aviation. The information technology sector became the poster child of Indian economic reforms, and grew by 30 per cent in the mid-1990s, creating several IT billionaires in its wake, too numerous to name but led by the storeyed rise of Infosys and its founders.

And fuelled by venture capital and rapid technological growth, we have new-age businesses, such as e-commerce company Flipkart, and online cab aggregator Ola.

References

Bhandari, Bhupesh. 'Once There Was the Bombay Club . . .', *Business Standard*, 8 July 2011, www.business-standard.com/article/opinion/bhupesh-bhandari-once-there-was-thebombay-club-111070800048_1.html.

GK Today. 'Industrial Policy Resolution 1956'. www.gktoday.in/industrial-policy-resolution-1956/#Schedule_B_Industries_as_per_Industrial_Policy_Resolution_1956.

Gupta, K.R. *Liberalisation and Globalisation of Indian Economy*, Volume III. New Delhi: Atlantic Publishers and Distributors, 1999.

Insights. 'Effects of Liberalization on Indian Economy and Society.' Insights on India, 14 December 2014, www.insightsonindia.com/2014/12/14/effects-liberalizationindian-economy-society/.

Khanna, Sundeep. 'How Liberalization Brought in a New Era for Business Families'. *Livemint*, 18 April 2016, www.livemint.com/Companies/WvQF2EW2xyOIKh2ey7bSQJ/Howliberalization-brought-in-a-new-era-for-business-familie.html.

Raghavan, T.C.A. Srinivasa. 'The Economic History of Liberation'. *Open*, 22 July 2016, www.openthemagazine.com/article/politics/the-economic-history-of-liberation.

Thakur, Anil Kumar, and Debes Mukhopadhayay. *Economic Philosophy of Jawaharlal Nehru*. New Delhi: Deep & Deep Publications, 2010.

7

SUCCESS AND CRASH

Whenever you think things are going well, take guard;
trouble is just around the corner.

We were on a roller-coaster ride, cresting great heights of success in the US before it came tumbling down on all fronts, at home and abroad. The years between 1991 and 2003 were bittersweet indeed.

The year 1991 began on a joyous note, with us having set a steady course for the Group the previous year. My heart was then filled with hope and renewed enthusiasm, and I wanted a bigger canvas to explore.

TTK Prestige was already the number one pressure cooker manufacturer in the world, and we had expanded into cookware. We were reasonably well established in the Indian market in the south and were gaining in the north, but organic growth had slowed down because of market saturation.

I set my sights on even higher growth for the company. Such a level of growth needed a larger market, and my thoughts turned to exports. America was the biggest market, and I wanted to be there.

Exploring America

I had an excellent resource by my side; with the reorganization of the Group and alignment of marketing functions with the respective companies, Nowroji's role as group marketing director had become redundant. I put him in charge of exports, and we began our foray into America.

We got a booth at National Houseware Show, the premier industry show, which was being held in Chicago in the freezing January of 1991. This was also the year of the first Gulf War. Its impact on the American economy would be felt much later, but it tipped the country into recession.

At the houseware show (now known as International Houseware Show), I was there to sell grills. Since Americans love barbecues, I felt that was the product for them. I didn't know that pressure cookers had a big market there until I saw them at the show. America seemed to be a logical choice for us to sell our cookers.

Nowroji recalls, 'We did our research on the US market and were surprised to find that pressure cookers had a significant $20–30-million market. This was due to the country's large Latin American population and their cooking habits. They cooked lots of meat and beans, which, cooked in the conventional way, would take thirty to forty minutes, whereas a pressure cooker could do it in ten minutes.

'The majority of the cookers in the US were from the Latin American countries. There was a Brazilian brand at the show and some Chinese cookers too.

'The US is a very difficult market to get into and has many requirements that we had to meet. We needed certification from the Underwriters Lab, without which we couldn't launch our product in the US. Product liability is a big issue there, and stores wouldn't touch our product if we didn't have insurance. Warehousing was another challenge, as stores didn't want to order a product in container loads. After much searching, we finally found a warehouse in New Orleans that was viable for us. It took two years to meet all these requirements and get everything in place, but our efforts paid off handsomely and we delivered a product that met the market's every requirement.

'The US market is also very unforgiving; you can't afford to make a mistake there as you will not be able to recover from it. None of our cookers ever had a problem; the Gasket Release System that we invented ensured that there wasn't a single safety incident.'

Brand Manttra

Sears, the well-known chain of department stores in the US, had its own store credit card and sent monthly bills to card holders. The envelopes in which the bills went out had discount offers, which were called 'envelope stuffers'. We had managed to get Sears interested in offering our cookers in these envelopes, but they needed a brand name.

We couldn't export under the Prestige brand anywhere outside India as the brand was owned by Meyer in America. We needed a new brand, and soon. I didn't want a Western-sounding name, I wanted it to be Indian. Over lunch at our head office in Bangalore, our top executives debated over the name when inspiration struck and a name for our new export brand flashed in my mind: 'Manttra'. The name reflected the brand's Indian origin and the 'tt' underlined the TTK connection.

National Houseware Show

By 1994–95, Manttra was moving well in the US. With certification, stock in the warehouse and in the stores, we did well at the Chicago shows, which were attended by every single buyer in the US.

We had started at the bottom in Chicago; our booth was in the basement. For the first four years I sat shivering in my booth, huddling in there to stay warm. Over time, we moved up levels to get to our current prime location.

I continued to visit the houseware show as a pilgrimage of sorts for fifteen years. Initially, though, we didn't bag orders, and it was only in our fifth year at the show that Macy's placed an order for Manttra cookers when one of its cooker suppliers couldn't deliver. There was no looking back after that, and all the other big chains—Walmart, KMart, Kohl's, JC Penney—followed, placing orders for our cookers.

Infomercials

Nowroji recalls, 'What helped us get our product into American stores were our infomercials. We were the first and perhaps the only cooker company to market and advertise pressure cookers; the other brands just had them on the shelves. We got a company headed by Bob Sterns to make infomercials in Spanish and English, which played a key role in the success of our product.

'We made three-minute videos, titled "Cook a Meal in Minutes", and launched a complete range of these programmes to communicate with the consumer. These had a chef cooking meat and beans and talking about pressure cooking being the healthiest way to cook. More importantly, we sold its convenience factor—of cooking meat and beans within minutes.

'Sales took off eventually, after many trips and many learnings. We had to change some specifications. Those days the cooker and the containers were both made of aluminium for the Indian market, but because of the Alzheimer's scare (which turned out to be a false alarm) we got our factories in India to make stainless steel containers for the US market. We also offered a pair of small steel tongs so the containers could be lifted out from the cooker and placed directly on the dining table.'

Million-dollar sales

I was passionate about Manttra Inc. and spearheaded the US operations personally. We set up a full-fledged sales network in the US, and between 1991 and 2009 we raked in $10 million in sales. In our best year we made $1.5 million.

By 2000, we had exported more than a million pressure cookers to the US, and these exports constituted nearly 50 per cent of our production. (Today, exports are 5 per cent of our production.) It is easier to do business in the US than in Europe as the US is the single largest market in the world with uniform standards.

While I led the Manttra expansion from the front, my second son, Lakshman, was also involved in Manttra Inc., which was run as a separate division. It had its own employees, and this company had to buy the products from Prestige, sell them in the US and make profits.

Market problems

Here is the story of Manttra in Lakshman's words:

'Manttra Inc. proved to be quite a challenge as we had to customize products for certain kinds of customers in the US and our factories in India had to redesign them. China was up and coming at the time, and Chinese products were sold at such low prices that it was hard to compete with them on cost price, though we could compete on features. Things began to get difficult as the big stores changed their merchandisers and buyers, who would in turn change their vendors.

'We were not a big brand in the US, and people didn't have any brand loyalty towards Manttra. Customers didn't specifically ask for our brand if they didn't find it in stock. We were stuck with products that we had made specially for a particular store and had to liquidate huge stocks at a loss. It was a very tough business for the margins that it made. It would probably have been viable if we had a vast product line which was not focused just on pressure cookers, as we do in India now.'

Small companies can easily be taken for a ride by large stores on various pretexts. We had some problems because their computers could not read the stickers on our boxes! That's how it works in America.

Bankruptcy

For ten years we had a great time and made a lot of money in the US, but when we shut down the American operations, we did so at a huge loss. There was a combination of reasons that led to our losses.

The market had begun to change; Walmart was destroying retail trade in a big way. It affected our customers who were big chain stores. Then the 9/11 terrorist attacks happened in the US in 2001. Together, these developments caused a dip in the US economy, and several of our customers went bankrupt, and that in turn made us bankrupt.

Our cookers continue to sell in the US, but we don't sell them directly. We supply to Meyer, and we earn only 30 per cent of the price as against the 60 per cent we were earning when we sold our own brand, Manttra. (A company has to pay stores a 40 per cent commission for stocking its brand; when it supplies a white-label product to another manufacturer/reseller, it earns much less.)

Life has always been interesting for me. Soon after the Manttra business ran aground in the US, we had more trouble, now at home.

Trouble comes in threes

A series of punches left Prestige reeling, almost knocking it down. In 2001, both the central and state governments levied duties that increased the tax on pressure cookers to 50 per cent (from 10 per cent). From being market leaders, we lost market share almost overnight to smaller players. The tax hurt not just us but all the other branded manufacturers of pressure cookers. Since the unorganized sector does not pay tax, the cost of cookers made by this sector remained the same while the cost of branded cookers went up.

Earlier, the price differential among the two sectors was just 10 per cent, and customers did not mind paying a little more for a branded product. But when the difference grew to 50 per cent, customers balked at the high price they had to pay for branded cookers.

All the companies in the organized sector lost money while the unorganized sector flourished. Over time, lobbying by the industry brought taxes down to 12 per cent as the pressure cooker had become an essential product.

Other companies in the TTK Group have also suffered because of unreasonable tax hikes. In 1979, Finance Minister Choudhury Charan Singh imposed 100 per cent tax on shaving cream and toothpaste, while exempting low-cost shaving kits from tax. We owned Williams shaving cream, having bought it through LJ Seymour from the US, and had been manufacturing it in Chennai. When the central tax alone was increased by 100 per cent—and we are not even considering state taxes here—we had to shut the business. At that time Rs 300 was a high price for a shaving cream; and people could do without shaving cream. The market just died. Again, we were the largest manufacturers of clocks. Our company, TimeAids, made West Clocks, but that business too died because of high taxes.

Wage agreement

It seemed that if anything could go against me, it did. While we were hit by a sudden slowdown of sales, we could not cut back on manufacturing thanks to a wage agreement with the workers. This agreement had been enforced to make the workers more productive, but as their pay depended on their producing a guaranteed number of units each day, the workers' union would not allow us to reduce the units being manufactured.

We went into a serious cash crisis as our factories kept producing products we couldn't sell. We were trying to get dealers to stock the products, but this led to increased credit, compounding our cash crunch. On the one hand, we were not able to collect money from the dealers, and on the other, we had to pay wages because our factories kept on producing goods. We had outstandings of more than eighty-eight months from the market. Credit was tight, and things were going to get worse.

Digging a hole

'I dug a deep hole for the company,' says S. Ravichandran, a former managing director of TTK Prestige. He refers to a brand-new product that tanked, nearly taking the company under with it. I will let Ravi tell this part of the story as he played a crucial role in digging the hole and in also getting the company out of it. Here it is, in his words:

'The "Smart" pressure cooker that we launched in 2001 was a beautiful, perfectly designed vessel. Until Smart came along, nothing much had changed in the pressure cooker market. There were only two kinds of pressure cookers: one kind with an outer lid and the other with an inner lid. Compared with these, Smart was a sophisticated product, with many interfaces, an automatic lock and three pressure modes. It could cook together various foods which require different cooking times, and release steam to make these adjustments.

'Smart was a revolutionary and modern product, and we decided to release it without a test launch. In hindsight, we ask ourselves why we did this. That was the time when we were starting to have growth pressures—the turnover had been flat at

Rs 100 crore ($15.5 million) for three years. The excise duty and sales tax were very high, and we couldn't counter the unorganized business, which was booming at the expense of organized players like us. We already had very high market shares in the metros, but the rural markets were very difficult to penetrate because the unorganized sector used different methods of selling there. We felt that unless we created excitement in the market, people would not exchange their old cookers for new ones or acquire a second pressure cooker.

'We were also supremely confident that the product would work. The technical team was confident that it was a fantastic product, and it worked perfectly in the lab and in beta tests.

'Chandru Kalro, the current managing director of the company, was the head of marketing then, and had prepared an aggressive and ambitious launch plan which included a package deal that offered one pressure cooker free to customers if they bought two.

'Chandru's plan was to sweep the trade off its feet because the market would never have seen anything like this. We thought we would very quickly establish the new product because of the brand's legacy. The buy-two-get-one-free offer would also remove any resistance to the new product, which was completely different from what consumers were used to. The strategy could not be faulted, as just one sale would allow us to get three cookers out into the market.

'None of us doubted the strategy. I was sold on it and approved it, and we went ahead to launch Smart cookers across all of India simultaneously. We had an eye-popping launch, for which we flew down dealers from all over India to Bangalore; and we took over half a dozen groups to Ooty for promotional activities over the next ten days.

'But the damned pressure cooker would not pressurize, and thousands of people who bought the cookers from our dealers across the country returned them as fast as they were sold. As we were to discover later, what failed in some of the cookers was a cast aluminium piece supplied by a vendor. This faulty piece prevented the cooker from pressurizing, and all the much-hyped features of separate release times for different foods were of no use when the cooker was unable to perform its basic function.

'The trade exploded; we had supplied 3,00,000 pressure cookers, and the dealers wanted to return all of them. Not all the Smart cookers had this problem, but customers who came to return their cookers would abuse the dealers, who in turn became upset with our company. We tried to fix it on the run, but the repair process took a few days, and that further annoyed the dealers. And sometimes, even the replacement cooker wouldn't work. The trade completely lost its cool and we were under intense pressure to collect all the cookers back.

'Chandru and his team, who were in touch with the dealers, reported the negative backlash in the market. It was unprecedented in TTK's history. It seemed that we had no road to travel, and I told TTJ, "Boss, I think we need to withdraw the product, correct it, test it, and see how to launch it again. But, for the moment, withdraw."

'We withdrew the Smart cooker, and in exchange we gave dealers our conventional pressure cookers. This further stressed manufacturing because the plants were geared to make the Smart cooker and had changed the manufacturing dimensions to suit the new product. Those are not days that any of us can recall without tremors even now.'

We had a great concept and fabulous promotion, but what failed was not the strategy or the design, but the manufacturing. This is a classic failure for a company.

We went on to export 5 million pieces of the same cooker later, but did not sell a single one in India. I tell my team that they are cowards, but Chandru's reply is, 'You don't even know about everything that happened, I have not told you everything. We can't launch it again.'

At that time, though, we were reeling under a series of severe blows: the market going bust in the US, the increase in taxes, the wage hike, the huge voluntary retirement scheme compensation to workers at the Bangalore factory and the failure of the much-hyped Smart cooker. The company was in deep trouble.

Sales dropped from Rs 141 crore ($22.2 million) in 1999–2000 to Rs 113 crore ($17.8 million) in 2002–03. We made a loss of Rs 36 crore ($5.6 million) and lost half our capital reserve. Our debt burden rose to Rs 80 crore ($12.6 million). I was gripped by the fear that this would surely be the end of TTK Prestige. What a sorry state of affairs for a company that had been making profits and paying dividends for forty straight years (from 1959–60 to 1999–2000)!

References

Economic Survey of India. 'Public Finance', 2004, http://www.indiabudget.gov.in/es2004-05/chapt2005/chapter2.pdf.

Notification. Department of Excise & Customs, Govt. of India, 1 March 2001, http://www.indiabudget.gov.in/ub2001-02/cen/cusnot17a.pdf.

'Speech of Shri Charan Singh, Deputy Prime Minister and Minister of Finance, Introducing the Budget for the Year 1979–80', http://www.indiabudget.gov.in/bspeech/bs197980.pdf.

8

TRANSFORMING TO TURNAROUND

Goal posts change, but the process of change remains.

We had our back to the wall, and we had to come out fighting. There was no other way, there was no doubt about that. From 2000 to 2003, the fortunes of the Group started to spiral downwards, and not just for Prestige. The other companies in the Group were flailing too. Our priority was our flagship Prestige, because if this one sank the whole pack of cards would collapse.

The sword of Damocles

Our first priority was to avoid coming under the purview of the Board for Industrial and Financial Reconstruction (BIFR), a body that had been set up by the central government in 1987 to address the spate of industries that had become sick. A company that lost more than 50 per cent of its capital reserves was deemed a fit case for BIFR.

The government in its wisdom would take over the running of the company, nominating to the board a director who was supposed to help sick units become productive. I don't think any company that came under BIFR was revived in this manner. The system was well-intentioned but badly executed. The government too realized this and shut down BIFR in 2016.

We had gone through a painful experience when our Group's hosiery company, Tantex, came under the purview of BIFR. The government-appointed nominee on our board was a bureaucrat and a friend. But he knew very little about business and could not help us turn it around. In the end, after a three-year struggle, we closed Tantex, a company that had been in business for twenty years.

There was a very real threat that Prestige too would come under BIFR, and we were determined not to let that happen. Fortunately, we stopped short of the line and we managed to avoid that calamity. Had we failed to do so, Prestige would not be the company it is today.

Transformation

What came to our aid was an exercise that we had embarked on in 2000. The company was stagnating, and I realized it was time that we shook ourselves up. While we had money, we were an also-ran company and weren't growing at the rate we should have been.

We had to change, as it was becoming more and more obvious to me that the problem was internal and not external. I don't believe in getting external consultants. The best way to change is to examine yourself honestly.

In June 2000, the entire company met at a resort in Mysore (now Mysuru) to deliberate the future. The programme was called

'Transform to Achieve', and we had focused on policy, strategy and the direction that Prestige would take. The whole company was involved in this soul-searching exercise. We had workshops and ideation sessions, and articulated a new vision statement that focused on maximizing the power of the TTK Prestige brand. We have had three such exercises so far. After the Mysore exercise in 2000, we had the 'Strategy to Excel' exercise in Kovalam in 2010 and the 'Total Transformation Exercise' in Hosur in 2015. These exercises have been very crucial to Prestige's growth.

These transformation programmes have led to changes in all aspects of the company—the manufacturing process, quality control, management, innovation, R&D and HR. We set up Centres of Excellence (CoEx) that meet every quarter to examine every aspect of the firm, to evaluate how things could be improved, and to set up cross-functional teams to implement the changes decided on. We continue to implement this programme. Though we have rectified everything that was wrong, we keep refining our processes.

By the time the Smart debacle happened, the seeds planted by the first transformation exercise had begun to show results. We had a brainstorming session to come up with a plan that would protect the company's future. With the entire company geared to tackle the challenge, we decided to focus on adding more products, gaining bigger market share and expanding our customer base.

Utilizing capital

Shankaran, group director, corporate affairs, says:

'We realized that there was a major problem in the way we utilized capital. Prestige had been a margin-led company, and we were passing on our inefficiency to the market. As a result, our products were overpriced all the time. We decided that margin would be a strategy for growth rather than an end in itself, and that we would employ capital more efficiently.'

Up to this time, I had thought that since we had a powerful brand we could charge high prices, which would give us high profits per piece sold. But there was some resistance in the market, and with dealers offering lower prices, their margins came down with the result that they sold fewer pieces. Our strategy had failed.

We reduced the margin sharply and began to make more money as the dealers sold more pieces. This is a learning that happened the hard way for me. We are still following the margin system that we established in 2003. The money we make has gone up. Those days our gross turnover was Rs 100 crore ($15.7 million), and our margin was 40 per cent of sales. We cut it to 20 per cent, and our gross turnover has grown to Rs 2000 crore ($315.4 million). From earning Rs 40 crore ($6.3 million) from a 40 per cent margin on Rs 100 crore in sales to earning Rs 400 crore ($63 million) from a 20 per cent margin on Rs 2000 crore ($315.4 million) in sales . . . the earnings difference is huge. We also tightened credit to the market, ensuring that the flow of revenue was even better.

We decided to close the factory in Bangalore as the cost of labour and lack of electricity had made it unaffordable for us to run it.

De-risking with breadth

Though we launched a new model of the traditional pressure cooker called 'Deluxe' within a month of the Smart cooker debacle, we also made a 'tectonic' shift from being just a pressure cooker company to sellers of a full range of equipment for the kitchen. Our opting for breadth came out of our learnings from the grave dangers that an increase in taxes had brought and the failure of our Smart cooker.

We had been overly dependent on cookers. By reducing our dependence on a single product, we could minimize risks for the company. We were determined that if something like a product collapse were to ever repeat, it would not pose as grave a hazard as it had before.

We ventured into cookware—stainless steel and non-stick vessels, and appliances. Until now we had only been selling what we made, but we discovered that the intrinsic power of the brand could be used to the maximum. We leveraged the strength of the Prestige brand and started sourcing products that we did not manufacture—such as stoves, small electrical kitchen appliances, mixer-grinders—selling them under our brand name. The addition of a range of appliances set us on a high-growth phase in 2003. We were confident that we had made the right move as we had a very good idea about what the customer wanted. Led by me, my senior team frequently explored the market and made sure they were clued-in on what would sell.

Sourcing imports

While we initially sourced the kitchen appliances from within India, we decided in 2005 to import them as we could get them cheaper and increase our range of products too. We commissioned sourcing capability checks on various manufacturers abroad, and after selecting the right vendors, we began importing rice cookers, toasters, kettles, induction cook-tops and a host of other such products. These were made to our specifications and sold under the Prestige brand.

There was more good news the same year. As the convener of the Pressure Cooker Industry Association, Shankaran led the industry talks with the government, persuading it to announce that the pressure cooker was not a luxury product. This was when the government reduced the tax on pressure cookers from 50 per cent to 12 per cent. This helped boost sales of our pressure cookers, and we regained our position as the market leader by 2005. We have never looked back since.

We set ourselves the objective of growing by 30 per cent year-on-year. It might have appeared an overambitious and even foolish objective, but we believed in ourselves and in the brand. The entire company was charged up and committed to meeting the target.

Our own shops

We were launching products at a feverish pace, but oddly enough, we found it difficult to distribute them. The big chain stores felt we were pressure cooker makers and did not want to stock our new range of electrical appliances. The *paatira kadais*, the traditional shops that sold humble kitchen utensils, did not want them either as they did not cater to a clientele that bought electrical appliances.

If nobody would sell our appliances, we would have to do it ourselves, we decided. That's when we hit upon the idea of starting our own stores. This posed a new challenge, as setting up stores would require a lot of investment. After some deliberation, we decided to adopt the franchise model, which saved us the huge investment we would have had to make in building a chain of stores. When we offered the franchise for Prestige Smart Kitchen stores, allowing franchisees to sell our growing range of cookers, cookware and kitchen appliances, applicants from across the country lined up eagerly, thanks to our strong brand name.

We started the sleek and colourful Prestige Smart Kitchen stores that stocked everything we made and sold, from cookers and cookware to a range of kitchen appliances. There was nothing like this in the market. 'Are you ready for a smarter kitchen?' was our new campaign as we launched kitchen appliances. The name Prestige Smart Kitchen lent itself perfectly to the business. The first Smart Kitchen franchise opened in Coimbatore and is still going strong. We now have 541 Smart Kitchen stores across 291 towns and cities. Fifty per cent of these stores are owned and very efficiently run by women.

The Smart Kitchen stores showcased our new products and transformed our ability to launch new products very quickly. We have been launching seventy-five to hundred new products almost every year since we established these stores. We are constantly in touch with the stores and have come up with several innovations based on customer feedback.

Dealer engagement

Would having our own stores affect our long-standing relationship with the trade? This was a key concern. Having been in the distribution business from the very inception of the company, we shared a good understanding with our network of dealers.

Ravichandran, who was then the managing director of the company, explains: 'After the failure of the Smart pressure cooker, our relationship with dealers became very different. We had taken back these cookers and replaced them with our regular cookers, ensuring that the dealers were not affected by our loss, and this had generated much goodwill. We had also consciously set about a very different kind of dealer engagement programme and we had become personal friends with our dealers.'

Chandru Kalro elaborates, 'We didn't want to upset or antagonize those who had supported us on our journey thus far. We also wanted to ensure that they did not cause a serious problem by putting a stop to the sale of our products altogether.

'We adopted a systematic approach to instil confidence among the dealers and reassure them that we were not competing with them. We held local dealer conferences in towns and cities to explain our business model. Whenever we opened a store in a town, our senior team would meet the dealers personally and invite them to dinner the evening before the launch of the store. Quite often, TTJ went along with me to invite them as he knew many of them from the early years.

'At these dinners, we explained the concept of the new store that we were launching the next day. We explained that the store would neither compete with theirs nor affect the key role their stores played in our business. We were there to launch new products, to convince them that these products were good enough for them to start stocking too. We also invited them to the store openings.

Latha and T.T. Jagannathan with grandchildren Rudro, Sarayu and Uma,
sons and daughters-in-law Venkatesh and Maitri, Lakshman and Shabari,
Mukund and Nidhishree

T.T. Jagannathan receiving the Business Standard Star SME Award in 2011
from the then prime minister Manmohan Singh

T.T. Raghunathan with wife, Bhanu, and son, Sriram

T.T. Jagannathan with the current MD, Chandru Kalro

T.T. Jagannathan receiving the TPM
Excellence Category A Award for the
Coimbatore plant from the Japan Institute of
Plant Maintenance in Kyoto in 2013. (inset)
Robotic cooker-top polishing in the plant

Aishwarya and Abhishek Bachchan reprise Prestige's signature line
'Jo biwi se karey pyaar, woh Prestige se kaise karey inkaar?'

TTK Prestige products (clockwise from top): Prestige Microchef-Microwaveable Pressure Cooker, Prestige Clip-on, Elegant Mixer Grinder, Prestige Hard-anodized Pressure Pan and Hero Electric Mop

Down memory lane · · ·

Shanthi Ranganathan is all smiles at Latha and T.T. Jagannathan's wedding

T.T. Ranganathan with his father, T.T. Narasimhan, and a guest

T.T. Jagannathan showing an award to his mother, Padma,
as his wife and father look on

T.T. Narasimhan, Padma Narasimhan and T.T. Jagannathan with top
executives of their joint venture partner, the London International Group

T.T. Jagannathan inking a deal with Maersk Medical's
Remy Cramer (extreme right)

T.T. Jagannathan, flanked by K. Shankaran, group director, corporate affairs,
and S. Ravichandran, then MD, at a dealers' conference

Nauzer Nowroji (extreme right), then marketing director,
TTK Group, at a meeting with T.T. Jagannathan

T.T. Jagannathan with his mother, Padma Narasimhan, at one of the
TTK Group factories in Virudhunagar

'We addressed a key worry—prices. We promised them that our stores would not undercut them and that our products would cost the same at our stores as in theirs. After their initial scepticism, the traders found that their business eventually increased, thanks to our stores. Customers would drop in at the Prestige Smart Kitchen stores to take a look at the host of new products available and would go back to their usual store to buy them. This helped us too as it pushed up sales.

'Another factor that helped push up sales was our launch of new and innovative products which the old stores did not stock at that point. When people visited the local stores asking for a new product, they had to place an order with us. The reality of business is that each time you launch something new, it opens up new business opportunities for many, improving business all around.

'This became a win–win for everybody, which is part of the culture of TTK Prestige. Our commitment to our associates' growth is our strong point and has helped us prevail over many competitors.'

A French suitor

Recovering after it hit rock bottom, the company had begun its climb up the J curve in 2004–05 (the fall and recovery of a company can be traced along the shape of the letter 'J'; the company, after making a recovery, reaches a higher point from where it had started out before its fall). It was around this time that, quite out of the blue, the French consortium Groupe SEB made an offer to buy Prestige. When Thierry de La Tour d'Artaise, chairman and chief executive officer of the company, asked for a meeting, I had no inkling that he would make such an offer. I am always open to meeting people, so I told him to come down to talk over a cup of good coffee.

When we met in my office, I was completely taken back by his offer, and my immediate reaction was one of indignation. I told him that we were not up for sale. But he asked that I hear him out, and the offer didn't seem too bad. In any case, I believe that one should not dismiss any offer outright.

We decided to consider it, and though I had mixed feelings, we held a workshop with our top management to discuss the pros and cons of the proposal. Ravichandran and Chandru began the process of business due diligence. As part of this process, they drew up an eight-year plan for the company.

We decided against the sale as this plan showed us the huge potential for growth that we had. We set about implementing the plan that had been so meticulously created. As Ravichandran says, 'The failed acquisition bid resulted in a template for our growth and made us think long-term.' We bested our eighth-year target in the fifth year itself, with aggressive growth in sales and introduction of new products. Groupe SEB did get into India a few years ago with some other brands, but have you ever heard of them? Our decision not to sell was right.

Conquering the north

Our next target was to expand our market base, which we did in 2006 by moving into the north, which was a bigger market than our stronghold in the south. Our team wanted to expand our reach across India but ran into a problem because north Indians wanted inner-lid cookers.

India's preference for cookers followed a geographical pattern. The south was happy with outer-lid cookers, the north chose inner-lid cookers and the middle was somewhere in between.

Prestige had specialized in making outer-lid cookers, which suited south Indian cooking. This design is more spacious, allowing for idli stands to be placed inside the cooker, or separators to cook rice, dal and vegetables. We had a share of between 80 per cent and 90 per cent of the outer-lid market, which was mostly in south India.

The outer-lid pressure cooker is British technology, while the inner-lid design is Brazilian. In terms of technology, inner-lid and outer-lid cookers are analogous to front-loading and top-loading washing machines, both serving the purpose of washing clothes. In America, all washing machines are top-loading, while in Europe they are front-loading. Perhaps these unique preferences grew from the earliest models that were available in those markets. Probably for the same reasons, south Indians like our outer-lid cookers whereas people in north India prefer inner-lid cookers, as the Hawkins pressure cooker maker was based in Punjab and made inner-lid cookers. North Indians also preferred the inner-lid cooker as they cook food directly in the cooker instead of in the separators.

Year after year, Ravichandran and Chandru would present their plan for an inner-lid cooker from Prestige, but for a long time I was reluctant to take up this design. But there was no disputing the fact that the north is a bigger market than the south. I was persuaded to admit that Prestige had to conquer the northern market. Our philosophy was simple: we are here to sell our customers what they want. If the customers in north India wanted the inner-lid pressure cooker, we were going to give them one.

Roorkee plant

Our plans for the north led to the setting up of Prestige's first factory outside south India—a separate factory, one that would make inner-lid cookers for the north Indian market. The state of Uttarakhand (Uttaranchal then) offered tax exemptions, and we set up a factory in Roorkee. To differentiate our products from those of our competitors, we launched inner-lid cookers with innovative shapes. One resembled a handi and another was apple-shaped. We launched both in 2006.

These products quickly powered our pan-India growth, and Prestige conquered the north–south divide, at least in the pressure cooker department.

Cookware

We had started manufacturing cookware in our Hosur factory, but demand soon outgrew the plant's capacity. The cookware market held enormous potential for growth, and I had great ambitions to tap it. We could make ten times the number of pieces (pots, frying pans and their ilk) of cookware with the capacity needed for a single pressure cooker. The cookware plant we set up in Hosur could produce 2800 pieces of cookware per day. Currently all our factories together have a production capacity of 30,000 pieces per day, or 9 million pieces a year.

Capitalizing on shortage

We expanded our range of kitchen appliances too. A little earlier, we had added gas stoves, small electrical appliances, mixer-grinders and food processors, which we imported and sold under the Prestige label. We introduced rice cookers, toasters and kettles too.

In 2009, when India had a shortage of the most common cooking fuel, liquefied petroleum gas (LPG), we came into the market with an induction stove. We sold a million pieces in the very first year. We added a host of cookware products for induction stoves and sold a million of those too.

In 2010–11, we adopted 'A Prestige in every kitchen' as our vision statement, and introduced a slew of products, such as high-end cookware, store ware, water filters and gas-tops, through alliances with several global brands.

Microwaveable pressure cooker, a global first

We launched Microchef, the world's first microwaveable pressure cooker, in 2011. It became an instant success abroad. Our export orders were huge. We export the microwaveable pressure cooker to every major country in the world. We sold a million in Japan in the first year alone. We hold many patents for this innovation, and we have been working on making it more acceptable to the Indian consumer.

In the years after the triple whammy brought Prestige to its knees, we had a period of steadying, consolidation and growth. We launched our own stores, started imports, launched more products, breached the north and set up new plants. More importantly, we were no longer just a pressure cooker company. We had shifted to a different zone, becoming a kitchen appliances company. While we still make 150 models of the pressure cooker today, they make up only 35 per cent of our turnover.

All this came about as a result of our clear focus on transformation as a continuing process. In 2003 we were worth about Rs 100 crore, and by 2013 we were worth Rs 1300 crore. By 2013, we had grown 27 per cent, pretty close to the high target of 30 per cent year-on-year growth that we had set for ourselves in 2003. Our share price went up from Rs 7 in 2003 to Rs 4000 in 2013. We became one of the most admired companies in the stock market too.

In keeping with our 2011 vision statement, 'A Prestige in every Indian kitchen', we also achieved brand recognition, winning our first Superbrand Award in 2006. Over the years we have got so many awards that our trophy cabinets have overflowed.

9

GROWING IN EUROPE
AND AT HOME

Keep your ego aside if you want to grow.

I am not usually a patient man, but experience has taught me to value patience. That's why I was able to wait ten long years to make another global foray after our derailment in America. Brands are where money is made; and it is the same thing with Prestige in India. The reason I am proud of the Prestige brand is that the consumer recognizes it as a trustworthy name. It's a trust that has been built over decades.

My ambition for a global presence for our own brand had continued to simmer, though the setback with Manttra Inc. in the US in 2000 made us cautious. After a ten-year search, we acquired UK's largest table and cookware suppliers, Horwood Homewares Ltd, in April 2016, and gained entry into the European market. TTK British Holdings is our overseas subsidiary that runs this business.

The Prestige brand

Prestige is a British brand. We had been using it to make pressure cookers in India from 1959. We bought the brand name in 1992, but our ownership of it is limited to India. We can't use the Prestige brand outside India. Though we export the cookers we make in India, the companies that buy them from us sell them under different names in different countries. This was the reason why we coined the brand name Manttra when we set out to sell our own brand in the US.

We had an opportunity to buy the global rights to the name when Prestige UK went bankrupt in 1991, closed its factories and put up the brand for auction. In those days of pre-liberalization, getting foreign exchange and permissions from RBI was mired in red tape. We were also a very small company then, with a turnover of just about Rs 10 crore. Despite that, we bid 6 million pounds, that is, about Rs 72 crore (the pound exchanged for Rs 12), which was a lot of money for a company our size. But I felt it was worth it as Prestige is a very powerful brand worldwide.

Outbid by the Chinese

We were outbid by the Meyer Group, a Chinese company based in Hong Kong, who bid 2 million pounds more than us for the brand. When the merchant banker asked if we wanted to top their bid we had to say no; 6 million pounds was the most we could extend ourselves to pay. We were then not the company that we are now, and I was worried about overextending ourselves.

I would buy the Prestige brand if it were to be available today. And I would be able to buy it without trouble as the situation in India is vastly different from what it was in the 1990s. Many merchant bankers will be eager to fund your brand purchase, whatever the price.

Though we lost the bid for worldwide use of the Prestige brand to the Chinese, I was thankful that I had had the foresight to buy the brand for India in 1992, or we would have been answering to the new Chinese owners.

The export market is not easy. We compete with the Chinese every day as they outbid us on price, especially in cookware. TTK Prestige's exports are largely white-label products to Meyer, which sells them around the world under the Prestige name.

But we cannot make as much money through white-label sales as we can if we sell our products under our own brand. This is how it works: if the retail price of a product is Rs 100, the distributor buys it from us at Rs 30 and sells it at Rs 60, as the stores usually take a 40 per cent margin. We have to manage raw material, manufacturing costs, depreciation, tooling and profit within the 30 per cent. If we sell our product ourselves, we can get twice this much, and our share would be 60 per cent of the sale price.

A suitable match

As Meyer has sole rights over the Prestige brand outside India, we had to have a different brand for the global market. I began to look out for an established brand. I could have started a new brand, but that would take its own time to succeed. For example, who would have thought a chocolate would be called Cadbury? But today chocolate is synonymous with Cadbury. One can always start a business, but it takes a long time to establish a brand. We did not have the money or the time to build a new global brand.

One has to be very careful while acquiring a business abroad. When we began to look for a suitable brand to buy, I had a few important stipulations. I had arrived at them after observing Indian industries that had tried to acquire foreign businesses and failed. If you look at the history of such acquisitions, a pattern is evident.

Firstly, they had bought loss-making companies. There are enough examples of Indian companies acquiring loss-making factories abroad and ending up selling them at a loss. Although, to be fair, it is only when companies start making losses that they are usually sold. Secondly, those companies were either of the same size or bigger than the parent company. Thirdly, there was no management left in the acquired companies.

Key conditions

Having analysed these acquisitions, I decided I would not repeat the same mistakes. I set four very specific conditions that the company we acquired had to meet. If it didn't satisfy these conditions, the brand we bought could drown us.

The first condition was that the company we acquire must be smaller than TTK Prestige; this would allow us to not only quit the business if it failed, but also ensure that its failure wouldn't affect our regular business.

The second condition was that it should be a profitable business. If it wasn't making profits, I wouldn't be able to guide it from India. It was important that it have a good management with whom I could work and help make more profits.

The third condition was that the company should have brands that were established in the world markets.

The fourth condition was that the company should not have its own manufacturing facilities. This condition was crucial, as we have seen the huge problems that come with purchase of manufacturing bases abroad.

Take the examples of the Mittals, who bought Arcelor, and the Tatas, who bought Corus. The Indian-owned multinational steel maker Mittal Steel took over European steel maker Arcelor in 2006. Over the years, ArcelorMittal announced several plant closures and laid off close to half its employees. It struggled with losses until 2016.[1]

The Indian multinational Tata Group acquired Corus Steel in 2007 and had a huge problem when it tried to close down Corus's manufacturing in the UK; Tata Steel Europe had a troubled innings, with prickly layoffs and mothballing

---

[1]   ArcelorMittal, 'Our History: ArcelorMittal', http://corporate. arcelormittal.com/who-we-are/our-history; Alan Tovey, 'Steel Crisis Spreads to Europe as Arcelor Mittal Shuts Spanish Plant', *Telegraph*, 25 January 2016, 'http://www.telegraph.co.uk/finance/ newsbysector/industry/12119963/Steel-crisis-spreads-to-Europe-as-Arcelor-Mittalshuts-Spanish-plant.html'; *IndustriALL*, 'ArcelorMittal Closes Plant in Trinidad & Tobago Leaving 600 Workers Unemployed', 30 March 2016, 'http://www.industriall-union.org/arcelormittal-closes-plant-intrinidad-tobago-leaving-600-workers-unemployed'; *Financial Times*, 'ArcelorMittal Shuts Part of French Plant', www.ft.com/content/fea87860-0bc2-11e2-b8d8-00144feabdc0.

or sale of plants. More recently, it merged its European steel business with the German steel manufacturer ThyssenKrupp, to form a joint venture named ThyssenKrupp Tata Steel. If the Tatas could not close manufacturing overseas, TTK certainly could not.[2]

Setting aside one's ego

Other Indian companies that had bought loss-making manufacturing companies that were bigger than themselves have suffered, and some of them have gone under. I do not want to name them as they are our direct competitors, except to say that I have learnt from their attempts at foreign acquisitions.

Unlike other Indian companies that aimed big, I wanted to make sure that our ego would not be part of the business decision; I was not interested in boasting about the size of the company we bought. Horwood is a very small company, but a very profitable one. It makes a 15 per cent return, and we are quite happy with its performance.

Retaining the team

The search for the right company took ten years. We finally decided on Horwood Homewares Ltd, which was owned by the UK holding of Portuguese stainless steel cookware

2   Inverandi, Matthias, Tom Kackenhoff, and Christoph Steitz, 'Thyssenkrupp, Workers Strike Deal on Tata Steel Europe Merger', *Livemint*, 23 December 2017. https://www.livemint.com/ Companies/qkVSYywj0zeXSnfxBpr0PI/Thyssenkrupp-workers- strike-deal-on-Tata-Steel-Europe-merge.html

manufacturer Silampos. Horwood is a century-old brand; it has been in operation since 1896 and is the largest table and cookware suppliers in the UK. It was a smaller company than ours. It did not have factories, but it had well-established brands. It has a strong brand equity and has experienced marketing, sales and distribution strengths. Horwood ticked all the boxes in my checklist.

One of our stipulations was that any company we acquired in Europe had to come with its management. It has taken us many years to learn how to run a business in India. I am now seventy, and cannot possibly learn how to run a business in England!

I was very impressed with the management at Horwood, and we have retained them. In fact, that was one of the conditions for our purchase. If the management had refused to stay, I would not have bought the company.

Investing in the acquisition

Horwood owns leading brands such as Judge, Stellar, Horwood and Kaffman, and also distributes other international brands, supplying over 2000 table and cookware products across Europe. The company had remained small only because its dividends and profits used to be taken by the parent company. The owners had a factory in Portugal making stainless steel cookware, which was making a loss. Horwood was put on the block to raise funds to rebuild the Portuguese company.

We are committed to building Horwood, and I have told them that for the first three years we don't want any dividend; they can keep the money to build the business. The management is thrilled with our decision; that was exactly what they had hoped for. When we first met them, their collective comment was to the effect that, 'If we had the money, the company would have grown bigger'. Now we are giving them the money to make it big. The new venture will combine the design, manufacturing and marketing capabilities of TTK Prestige to expand and grow its business in the European markets.

TTK Prestige acquired 100 per cent of the equity shares of Silampos UK Ltd, based in Bristol, and through this company acquired 100 per cent of the equity and business of Horwood Homewares Ltd. We set up an overseas subsidiary, TTK British Holdings, to run this business.

The stock market greeted this acquisition extremely well. Leading financial firms recommended that investors buy the stock of TTK Prestige. Our share price, which was a little over Rs 4000 at that time, began rising steadily (it soared past Rs 7000 in late 2017).

Global edge

This acquisition has given TTK Prestige an opportunity to re-enter the global market, and we plan to take advantage of Horwood's network of over 1000 retailers. Apart from using the untapped capacity of our production facilities in India to supply to Horwood, we stand to also benefit from the higher pricing that is possible in Europe.

We have begun supplying pressure cookers to Horwood, to be sold under its top two brands, Judge and Stellar. Currently, Horwood buys most of its goods from China and sells them at a profitable price. We don't want to change that, as it would be foolish to try to make a little more money here for Prestige and lose the bigger profits from Horwood. So Horwood will continue to buy from China, and we will keep adding to it different lines of products from India, such as cookware.

We have given Horwood funds to enter Europe. We also gave it our booth at the International Houseware Show in the US. The location of an exhibitor's booth at the show is very important; it improves with the seniority of the participant. TTK Prestige has worked its way up to an ideal location as we have been there for twenty-five years. Since we don't have a brand in the US any more, we decided to let Horwood use our booth to establish their brands. Americans like British names, you see, and the company had a reasonably good show in Chicago.

We have already started looking to expand the brand into the US, Australia, New Zealand and Europe. In 2017, we gave Horwood TTK's stall at the Ambiente, one of the world's most important consumer goods trade fair in Frankfurt, and the business was very good.

We were using the Manttra brand for many of our exports. For instance, if someone in Africa who does not have their own brand asked for a pressure cooker, we sold it to them under the Manttra band. But we want to popularize Judge and now use this name instead. We have already got two distributors in the Middle East for Judge, and we will start exporting from here.

Competing at home

We now have more competitors than ever before, and this is because we are now in varied markets. Not only did we add wired business to our non-wired business, we have also moved from the kitchen to the home.

The business has to be growing all the time. Growth is the only constant, and we can't afford to be complacent.

Wired and non-wired

Chandru Kalro says, 'We are always looking for new avenues for growth, and we made a breakthrough with electrical appliances. In India, we are far ahead of the competition in our traditional business of pressure cookers, with our closest rival being half our size. But we have many more rivals because we are also in the electrical appliances business. This puts Prestige in a class by itself, as the only company with a countrywide presence in both non-electrical and electrical domestic kitchen appliances. This has pitted us against several other competitors. Apart from Hawkins in the pressure cooker segment, we now have Bajaj, Philips, Havells and many more competitors in the electrical segment.

The inclusion of electrics, or wired, to non-electrics, or non-wired, is a major addition for the company, and is not easy. The consumer does not necessarily trust your capabilities in electrical appliances just because you are a good player in non-electrical appliances; in fact, for this very reason they might be sceptical. Not everyone has done such an expansion successfully, but we have.

Six million homes

We have also adopted new sales models, and Prestige is now in 6 million Indian households. In the last decade and a half, our distribution has expanded in width and depth. We are in every format of selling. We are the most widely distributed brand through traditional outlets. Our products are sold in over 65,000 outlets across the country; we are available even in towns with populations of just 50,000.

Apart from our 541 exclusive Prestige Smart Kitchen stores, we sell through all the retail chains and to institutions too. We were among the earlier adopters of online selling. We sell on our own website, as well as on all online platforms. Close to 5 per cent of our revenues comes from online sales.

We work with microfinance companies to sell in rural areas. In the villages, we have women selling our products to their fellow villagers. We have learnt that the ambitions of our rural customers are pretty much the same as those of their urban counterparts. In fact, people in rural areas have higher disposable incomes because they do not have many avenues for spending. With the proliferation of media, everybody everywhere is exposed to every new product and wants everything.

From the kitchen to the home

Kalro has this to say about the new direction that Prestige has taken: 'After transforming the way India cooks, Prestige is also transforming the way India cleans. We launched the Clean Home range of products in 2016.

'We sell almost every product used in the kitchen. We could see that organic growth could be quite small. Complacency kills, and I knew we had to bring out new products and be ahead of the game. We had to broaden our portfolio, and the natural extension seemed to be from the kitchen to the home. There are excellent prospects for growth here as the market opportunity in the home cleaning segment is Rs 2500 crore and growing.'

Competition is fierce in the consumer durables business, so we had to be very careful in selecting the areas we were entering. We picked cleaning solutions for three reasons: first, the consumer segment would be the same—the homemaker who was already familiar with Prestige and trusted the brand; second, we could use the same distribution channels we did for kitchenware; and third, we had developed in-house the world's first domestic electric mop, for which we have a patent.

We launched the Prestige Clean Home range with the slogan 'Don't touch the dirt, don't spread the dirt'. We have fifty products, both electric and non-electric, to clean everything in the home from the air to the floor—from mops to window cleaners to ladders and flip bins. We have already won design awards for three of our products. In December 2017 we launched two exciting new products. A mop in India generally only redistributes the dirt, but our Hero electric mop is very thorough and removes all the dirt from the floor. We also launched the Tattva non-electric water purifier, which works on the principle of gravity.

Prestige Clean Home is our next big push for growth. We expect it to contribute 8–10 per cent of our revenue in the next three years, and there's a great export market for this range too.

10A

COOKING UP INVENTIONS

If you take the market for granted, very quickly everybody has caught up with you, and you find yourself losing market share.

In the words of Latha Jagannathan: 'Jaggu enjoys everything that he does. It could be playing a game with us, cooking bondas or making some changes to the pressure cooker. He puts in the same amount of energy and enthusiasm into everything.'

One of the key drivers of Prestige's success is continual innovation; our budget for innovation and development is about 1.5 per cent of our sales. Our innovations are also a coming together of my twin passions of cooking and engineering. I often wonder if the many inventions that Prestige has pioneered would have happened had I not been a keen chef. That is a question I cannot answer definitively.

I do know that as a mechanical engineer I was able to come up with products and solutions. After inventing the GRS that stopped pressure cookers from bursting in 1981, I set up a full-fledged product development department. A culture of innovation became part of TTK's DNA from thereon.

The product development department in Hosur has been the cradle of many innovations, including the pressure pan. This was the first indigenous product we developed, and it was a game changer. This invention happened because I cook a lot and am also eager to see what and how others cook. I noticed that many people were using the cooker vessel to sauté or fry vegetables or meat before pressure-cooking them. It then occurred to me that we could make a vessel that was more suited to Indian cooking. The result of this was the pressure pan, which was ideal for cooking all the typical Indian foods that need seasoning, such as vegetable, chicken and meat dishes in gravy. The consumers loved it when we later introduced a combination package, offering a pressure cooker and a pressure pan with a common lid for both.

A 'frying' success

As an inventor, I am influenced by my own experiences, and I try to make things easier for others who may be having the same experiences. I remember the days when my wife and I used to make *karuvadam* and *vadam* (south Indian papads) at home each year in February, because that was the only month when it wouldn't rain in Bangalore (though climate change has changed the rainfall pattern now). The traditional method of extruding the dough was back-breaking work; we had to push the dough manually through perforated plates before spreading the papads out to dry on the rooftop, and guard them against birds and the rain. In my parents' home in Madras, there was plenty of domestic help; but when we moved to Bangalore, Latha and I couldn't afford extra help.

A few years later, it occurred to me that the process of extrusion could be mechanized. This papad-like snack was very popular, and I felt it could be a big business. I went to Italy to buy a pasta machine. Essentially, the machine is fed with a dough of white flour, which it extrudes in different shapes—for example, macaroni, spaghetti, farfalle and so on. The pasta machines didn't have a gelatinizer, though.

Gelatinizing does not involve gelatin; it is a term for the process of cooking starch. When you stir up a pot of maida, it acquires a gooey texture; this is the gelatinized starch that is extruded through a press. It is an important step in making the south Indian papads that I wanted.

Pasta doesn't need to be gelatinized, so the Italian machines did not come with a gelatinizer. But the Italians did have a separate gelatinizer, so I took that, attached it to the pasta machine, gelatinized the starch, extruded it, cut it and produced what we called 'Fryums'. We launched Fryums in 1990, and look at the success that it is! (See Chapter 13: Skore and More.)

A solution, not a product

My grandfather, T.T. Krishnamachari, sowed the seeds of the TTK Group's success by personally travelling to towns and cities, and meeting dealers, retailers and customers. My father, T.T. Narasimhan, continued this practice. I learnt the importance of the need to personally meet our customers when I took charge at TTK Prestige. Had I not gone out into the streets to see why our cookers were not selling as well as they ought to have been in the northern markets, the issue of the spurious parts that were the cause of our cookers bursting would not have come to light.

The fact that we are in constant touch with the market has proved helpful, time and again. A consumer cannot tell you what she wants, but she can tell you what she doesn't like and what she has a problem with. I like to look at the pain points of the consumer and offer solutions.

Take induction cooktops, for example. We were not the first to launch them. We launched ours in 2009, at a critical time when there was shortage of LPG, which was the popular cooking fuel. Though the technology was safer and more efficient, we found that people weren't buying induction cooktops because they didn't have utensils that could work on them.

We came up with the perfect solution: since we were already in the business of making non-stick cookware, we now made them induction-friendly. We bundled this cookware along with induction cooktops, and sales zoomed. For the customers, it was a simple plug-and-play; our bundled solution allowed them to start using the cooktop and cookware right away. It was a very simple putting together of two capabilities, and our sales grew by 60 per cent. To make customers adapt to induction cooktops, we stopped selling them as products but offered them as a solution.

Next, we tweaked the design of the induction cooktop. Originally, it had been designed for Chinese cooking, which involves stir-frying for three minutes and no more. Indian cooking is not about three minutes of stir-frying. It's about frying, sautéing and pressure-cooking. Many more processes go into Indian cuisine. We realized that we had to sell a product that could run trouble-free for thirty minutes and also be a solution for regular Indian cooking needs.

We decided to redesign the induction cooktop for longer cooking cycles. We put menus inside the induction cooktop for deep-fried, pressure-cooked and sautéd dishes, including all the processes that a normal Indian kitchen employs.

We also added a second sensor to make sure that the temperatures were controlled and that the stove would run for thirty minutes. For example, we ensured that deep-frying was enabled at 180°C. We got deep into the details. And the benefit is that when you deep-fry food using an induction cooker, the temperature is controlled and the food is healthier than the deep-fried food made in an uncontrolled, smoky kadai which carbonizes the oil. Our customers appreciate the value addition that we give to our products.

The clip-on cooker

Another major achievement was the clip-on pressure cooker that we launched in 2016. It's been doing much better than we expected, as the cooker can be moved from the stove to the dining table. What's more, the clip-on cooker lid fits any Prestige vessel—our handis, kadais and saucepans. These are the kinds of innovation that the market loves, and we love serving them up too.

Inventing a pressure cooker for the microwave

We spent five years inventing and developing the world's first microwaveable pressure cooker and the world's first electric mop.

The microwaveable pressure cooker cooks very fast, as the food starts to cook as soon as the microwave facility is turned on. In conventional cookers, the water has to start to boil before the cooking process starts.

We made a microwaveable pressure cooker for a very simple reason. Typically, people use the microwave oven just for reheating food. I thought that if we could make a pressure cooker that cooks in the microwave oven, it would utilize the oven better, leaving one stovetop burner free for cooking other food. The microwave cooker is also better than an automatic rice cooker, which only cooks rice. You can't cook meat in a rice cooker.

Our microwave pressure cooker is fully automatic, simply because the microwave oven is automatic. You can set the time and go away while it cooks your food, after which it will keep it warm. The taste of vegetables and meat from this method of cooking is fantastic, and we have been exporting over a million pieces a year to Japan alone, apart from selling in the US, UK and Germany. The Indian market has been resistant to it, though. We have been working on a solution and are close to a breakthrough.

Microwaveable coffee maker

We are currently working on a microwaveable coffee maker. Good coffee needs pressure; all Italian coffees are made in pressure machines. We are experts in pressure, after all, and it occurred to me that we could combine this with the expertise we had gained in making the microwaveable cooker to make a microwaveable coffee maker. It's nearly ready, and we are working on fine-tuning a few small details.

Mopping up

The electric mop that we launched in 2016 came about because I hated mopping the house whenever the maid didn't turn up for the day. A few years ago I decided that I would create a mop. It took five years to develop it from the idea to the product stage. It is a deep-cleaning product that sweeps, scrubs, mops and dries the floor.

Launch pad Bengaluru

We always launch all our products in Bengaluru, apart from one other city, which we choose depending on the product. We don't do national launches as there are always glitches in a new product. We limit our launches, wait for feedback, make rectifications if they are needed and then send out our products. This is the lesson we learnt from the Smart pressure cooker's national launch and the storm it caused when the product failed.

Apart from being the headquarters of TTK Prestige, Bengaluru is a great launch pad for new products. We can reach a wider cross-section of people because of its cosmopolitan population, and the city has a large number of techies who are highly articulate and give us valuable feedback.

Tool room and product development lab

We also make our own tools, and we have a very sophisticated tool room for this in Hosur. We set it up in 1987 at a cost of Rs 4 crore. This was a very expensive investment at the time, when our turnover was just Rs 25 crore. But I felt that if we had to get into exports in a big way, we would need a tool room. The maintenance tool room that we had earlier made one or two tools a year. Now we make a couple of tools a day as we do a lot of customization. Each person in the tool room knows how to handle each of the machines, and work is not affected if any among the staff is absent. After we set up the very fancy tool room, we created the product development lab, which has a separate, dedicated space. This was created after my first invention (the GRS), when I gained the confidence that I could do something better than just make standard pressure cookers.

I am passionate about product development; there's nothing I like more than to go to the lab and test our new products. This is the only department in which I am still very actively involved, and I go to the product development lab in Hosur on Saturdays whenever I am in Bengaluru.

We have a very good team of engineers in this department. Our innovations are triggered by our visits to the major global trade shows. Even our pressure cookers are always innovative, and no design is older than five years. We customize our products by creating different sizes, shapes and appearances. We make 140 different types of the pressure cooker alone. Even the cookers we export are different; we make a different design for each buyer if we have more than one buyer in the same country or market.

R&D

Research and development plays a key role at our company, and this division creates focus groups for consumer insights, surveys and feedback. We also have internal brainstorming sessions.

We have an innovation theme that encourages our people to contribute suggestions on the company's intranet. Any employee can send in a suggestion, which then gets reviewed. We get forty to fifty suggestions a month. We also get suggestions from our consumers who log on to our website and suggest innovations. We study their suggestions and remove their pain points with respect to our products.

As I have said earlier, we visit the major trade shows in Frankfurt, China and the US, and pick up ideas from there. We study the feasibility of these ideas and get design reviews done. The marketing team gives its inputs too. Ours is a very systematic way of approving innovations, and any new idea that appears to have a business possibility moves to the design brief stage, going through reviews, prototypes, costing and, finally, mass manufacture.

Development cycle

The product development cycle for some projects can be quite long. Our domestic electric mop, the Hero, was five years in the making. We started work on the microwaveable pressure cooker in 2005, and it went through many iterations before we finished it in 2011. It was very difficult to design, and we burst many microwaves in the initial stages of its development.

Getting the process right was a challenge because we were moving from metal to composite. We were experts in metal, and handling composites was a big task. It required a lot of study and change. We have mastered it now and have many global patents for the microwaveable pressure cooker.

Water purifier

The Tattva water purifier is a unique blend of tradition and modernity, and it grew out of our experience with an earlier water purifier with a different technology.

During 2012–14, TTK Prestige had tied up with Switzerland's Vestergaard Frandsen and introduced a water purifier with state-of-the-art technology. Called Prestige LifeStraw, it had a chemical-free purification process and retained all the essential minerals in the water. It was an excellent product and met stringent US Environment Protection Agency (EPA) standards.

We realized within the first three months of its launch that we had misread the market. The technology was great but the product was too expensive for the Indian market. We had intense competition from HUL (whose water filter used chlorine and was priced much cheaper). We discussed the problems with Vestergaard and we parted ways amicably.

As part of that learning experience, we figured out that we could make a much cheaper and superior water purifier. We have worked on a very different kind of water purifier, and have launched gravity water filters that incorporate traditional Indian preferences.

Tattva has the largest range of gravity water purifiers in the non-electric segment in India. It has a natural, advanced FACT (Fibrillated Adsorbent Cellulose Technology) filter that removes harmful bacteria, protozoa and cysts from the water to make it safe and clean. The three-stage filtration using chemical-free purification technology can purify nine litres of water every hour and meets US EPA standards.

Tattva is easy to use. The owner can herself change the filter cartridge every six months. Infusing a touch of traditional Indian values, the containers are also available in copper and brass.

Adapting to the new

Our customers are changing, and so are their needs. We want to ensure that we have something for everybody.

From heart-shaped idli moulds to onion slicers and atta kneaders, from ladders with seats to knives that don't lose their sharpness, we try to address all the desires and needs of our customers. We have a scientific approach to the products we manufacture or sell. We will keep brainstorming to see what problems we can solve and what needs we can meet next.

Homes and kitchens have changed in the way they are designed and used. They have 'open plans' and are no longer only a woman's domain. Husbands and children play active roles in there too, and we sell smart products that everybody can use.

Awards

We are proud that our innovations have been winning design awards. Our award-winning hob-top is on permanent display at the Henry Ford Museum in Michigan.

We have won several awards for design and development. Some of them are:

- International Design Excellence Award (IDEA) for the hob-top by Industrial Designers Society of America
- India Design Mark for the hob-top and the clip-on cooker
- CII Best Design award for the clip-on cooker
- European Design award for the hob-top and the clip-on cooker
- Elle Décor best design award for the apple cookers
- Best of All—Red Dot award in Germany for the hob-top

Brand awards

The TTK brand has been winning ten to fifteen awards each year for the last decade. Some of the major awards the brand has won are:

+ Superbrand—for six consecutive years
+ India's Most Trusted Brand Award—three times running
+ Master Brand—four times in a row
+ Franchisor of the year—Home/Home Products category by the Franchise Awards 2016
+ CNN India's Most Admired Brands and Leaders Award
+ Times Ascent 'Dream Companies to Work for' Award
+ CXELA Best After Sales Service—Small & Kitchen Appliance Company

The big awards the company is particularly proud of are:

+ Best SME Award (out of 4 lakh SMEs) that I received from the prime minister
+ Total Productive Maintenance Award from JIPM, Japan—first in the consumer durables industry
+ A personal award from E&Y as entrepreneur of the year (for consumer products)

10B

A COOK IN THE TOP JOB

To cook well you have to practise cooking.

I was the daughter that my parents never had. I learnt to cook, knit, sew and play the violin. I did all the things that normally a daughter would do in a south Indian family.

Mother herself didn't knit, cook or sew, but as I was very fidgety—and to keep my fingers from getting into other things—she got someone to teach me knitting. I don't understand why it's considered a suitable activity for women but not for men. Where have all these rules come from?

I learnt sewing on my own; you can pick up anything if you are interested in it. What is so difficult about it? You take two pieces of cloth and put them in a machine; or you cut the cloth and hem it. I used to stitch things for the house—cushion covers, pillow cases and other simple stuff.

When our eldest son was born, I got a Singer sewing machine and sewed his entire wardrobe—his pillows, pillow cases, bed sheets and clothes. He was born three weeks early and I was not ready with his clothes, so I told Latha to spend a few extra days in the hospital while I finished the clothes.

Learning to cook

I started cooking at the age of eight. My mother didn't know how to cook, and at home in Madras the kitchen belonged to our cook, Paramashivam. He was our Anatole, the best cook in the world, and my friends used to come home from the hostel even when I wasn't at home to eat their fill. He made simple south Indian fare like idli and dosa, but his food was outstanding. He didn't use any measures; I was fascinated by his style of cooking, and I started to learn to cook by watching him.

I was not allowed to do anything more than dabble in the kitchen, of course, and it was only in the US that I began to cook regularly. We were vegetarian at home, and I was one too till my final year at IIT. When I got admission in Cornell University, people told that me that I would not survive in the US if I were to remain a vegetarian. I tried chicken in IIT Madras, but it was awful and I decided that I was not going to become a non-vegetarian.

When I went to America in the 1970s, unlike now, when there are Indian restaurants in every college or town, there weren't any. After two weeks in the country I started to cook my own food. I also became a non-vegetarian there, as I liked hamburgers, hot dogs and steaks. Even today, I prefer meat cooked in the Western style.

I love cooking; I cook for myself, my family, my friends and my colleagues. I learnt how to use a pressure cooker from my mother-in-law. I like going to the shops to buy ingredients, but I can cook with whatever is available. We usually eat south Indian every day, and occasionally make pasta or something different.

I taught Latha, my wife, to cook. Having lived in hostels, she hadn't learnt to cook. When we set up home in Bangalore, Father used to come and stay with us when he was here for the races. On one such visit, the cook and Latha had a falling out and Latha sacked him. Her problem was that he had not readied lunch in time, and Father needed to eat before he left for the races.

She called me in a panic. Our home was then in Indiranagar. In those days there was hardly any traffic on the roads, and I drove home from the factory in Doorvaninagar in a very short time and cooked a meal. Over the next couple of months, I taught Latha to cook.

My sons learnt to cook from me. It was something they picked up by just watching me. I used to visit them often when they were studying in the US and cook for them. While Lakshman and Venkatesh are both excellent cooks, my eldest son, Mukund, is not so keen on it. I remember his calling me once on the phone asking me to take him through the process of making potato curry. I told him to practise; cooking comes only by practice. You can read any number of books but you have to practise, tasting your creation from time to time.

Appa in the kitchen

'One does not cook with Appa, in the same way that one does not fly a kite in a tornado,' says Venkatesh. 'He's a force of nature in the kitchen. And all four of us are too opinionated to be able to cook together. Too many cooks . . .

'What he taught us was "formula cooking". Chicken curries start with frying onions, adding the spices, adding the chicken, the veggies, the liquid you chose, and simmering it all. Whether you wanted it green, red, brown, thick, thin, with coconut milk, curd, coriander . . . all that was flexible. The same rules went for dal and most TamBrahm food. I remember holidays being the time he cooked the most, because he was usually too busy otherwise to cook at home on a regular basis.

'When I was in Cornell, he bought me a few pans and oil, spices, etc., then told me I'd figure out cooking by myself. I ate really bad food for a year. I remember making a lot of phone calls clarifying cooking methods with him. There were never recipes coming from him because there were never any specified quantities. He would say, "Now put in some mustard and fry it till it crackles." Most importantly, he taught us that a good cook can use whatever is available in the pantry to make a good dish. Don't blame anything on the lack of ingredients.

'Whenever he came, there would always be many friends invited over for meals. And he'd cook up a storm, usually leaving a trail of destruction in his path. While he is an excellent cook, he is terrible at keeping the kitchen clean while cooking.'

Appa cake

'For all our birthdays he always baked his special cake, which came to be known as "Appa cake",' recalls Mukund. 'The tradition still continues, but now it's called "Thatha cake" (Grandfather cake). The secret was to use Bournvita powder instead of chocolate; I don't really know how that got started.

'His specialty was to see what's in the fridge and pantry and then whip up a meal. I remember learning to cook chicken curry—one of the earliest dishes I learnt. All in a single pressure cooker. Fry everything, masala, chicken, close the vessel, and you are good to go. My housemates in Boston, while I was at MIT, loved the chicken he'd cook whenever he visited. I remember that one time it was quite a bit spicier than we usually make it at home and they kept asking for more.'

Company of cooks

Undoubtedly, a passion for cooking drives me and our top managers. While I don't have an answer to the question of whether Prestige would have been as successful as it is today had I not been interested in cooking, Chandru is quite clear that a love for cooking plays an important role. 'You're not likely to be successful in this industry if you didn't know to cook, if you didn't cook and if you didn't love cooking. If I am going to talk to customers about their problems, unless I know cooking and I like cooking and also cook, I won't be able to even understand what they are saying. So it is important for us to be able to cook and gain an understanding of different cuisines.'

When we travel together we typically don't stay in a hotel. We stay in an apartment and cook our dinner ourselves. It is a nice bonding activity, with all of us taking turns to cook each day.

Have we helped many more men become good cooks? We can't take any credit for this. It is certainly their wives or mothers who have to turn them into good cooks. But we as a company have certainly made cooking easier.

11

MANUFACTURING INNOVATION

*Investing cash to expand your business is better
than keeping money in the bank.*

One day, sometime in 2010–11, Ravichandran, then MD of our company, walked into my office to declare, 'We have got money in the bank.' I knew that, of course, and said so. He went on to say, 'Let me use that money. You will have double by the end of the year.' By the next year, he said, we would have close to four times the amount in the bank. He wanted us to build new factories to increase our production capacity and earn huge revenues.

If we wanted to go global, as we did, we would have to invest in new factories. To become global, we must have global quality and global manufacturing in terms of scale, and the equipment that produced the right quality. Compared with the huge automatic plants in China, Indian factories were cow sheds, Ravichandran pointed out.

We invested close to Rs 350 crore ($55.1 million) in manufacturing between 2010 and 2014. We undertook extensive and expensive plant expansion and modernization in both Coimbatore and Roorkee. In 2011 we also embarked on our largest capacity expansion, setting up a new factory in Karjan, Gujarat, and buying another in Khardi, Maharashtra, thereby doubling our manufacturing capacities.

Making money work

When we began expanding capacity, we were flush with cash, having accumulated Rs 200 crore ($31.5 million) in the bank. But our expansions cost us Rs 450 crore ($70.9 million), more than double of what we had planned, and we were back in debt. To be fair, the plant in Karjan was not part of the original plan at all, and this by itself cost Rs 150 crore ($23.6 million). The company had become cash-positive about five years ago, after which we had bought Horwood, turning the company cash-negative again. As of now, we are sitting on Rs 200 crore ($31.5 million) and I am waiting for my MD to come and tell me that he wants Rs 100 crore ($15.7 million). It will happen. It's a cycle. Cash in the bank is wasted as it earns you interest of only 5 per cent, whereas returns from business amount to 30 per cent.

The plus about the factory expansion and modernization is that we won't need to make major capital expenditure in the near future as we have created capacities that can handle increased production in proportion to our envisaged growth.

Robots at work

Each month, 700 tonnes of aluminium circles and 120 tonnes of steel arrive at our five factories, where the manufacturing units set about making pressure cookers, pans and a whole range of cookware out of them.

Two of our factories, in Karjan in Gujarat and in Coimbatore in Tamil Nadu, are industry showpieces as they are completely automated. The sophisticated manufacture of anodized pressure cookers and cookware using robots is the subject of a programme on Discovery channel.

The factories and their processes have come a long way indeed from the very first unit my father set up in Bangalore in 1959, though for those times it was a state-of-the-art plant.

Innovating processes

Along with modernization, we have been innovating manufacturing technologies and processes too. I was keen to improve the processes from the time I took over Prestige. In the seventies, each worker produced approximately two cookers a day. Today we make forty-eight pressure cookers per worker per day.

The manufacture of a pressure cooker involves various operations. There are three main processes: draw, trim and fold. The major process is cup-drawing, in which a stainless steel disc is drawn through an inverted circular-shaped die to form a round pot, which is the body of the cooker. The lid-making too involves several operations before which it comes to the assembly line. Here the processes are polishing, piercing, riveting, fixing of handles, attaching of the weight valve, the safety plug, the gasket and so on, all the way to the packaging of the cooker.

From batch to line

The factory practised a system called 'batch processing' to carry out all of the above tasks. This process involved about ten groups of workers in the factory, each doing a particular job at a time. For example, to make 100 cookers, the first group would press 100 pieces of metal and pass them on to the next group, which would do the secondary operation. The 100 cookers would go from group to group, each group performing a particular function. It was a highly inefficient process.

'Line manufacturing' is a far more efficient system. It was pioneered by Henry Ford way back in the 1800s. Also called the 'single-piece flow' system, it is far more efficient in production facilities and had changed the nature of manufacturing. It was a proven technology, but even in 1975 our factory followed the old and inefficient batch system.

When I took charge at Prestige and wanted to change the manufacturing process, the employees were opposed to it. Holding on to received wisdom, they resisted any change as they felt that the technology that had come from UK should not be meddled with. We were making cookers the same way Ambassador and Premier Padmini cars were being made in India, without changing anything from the time their making began!

After I had worked at Prestige for a couple of years and won the workers' trust by getting the factory a quota of aluminium that got it running again, the staff began to trust me. This time I was able to take over the entire engineering portfolio, and I moved our manufacturing from batch process to line process. We keep improving the process continually. Various functions of the line process need to be automated and updated every year.

For example, polishing, which used to be carried out manually, is now done by machines.

I set up a line system in Prestige in the eighties. This meant that instead of a whole set of cookers moving from one operation to the next, a single unit keeps moving down the line. The first person rivets the brackets, after which the product immediately goes to the next person waiting to do the next job in the line, and so on. While we have workers in our second oldest factory in Hosur, we use robots in the Coimbatore and Karjan factories.

A breakthrough invention

We have achieved something remarkable at our factory in Coimbatore. We used to make aluminium cookers here, and the factory had mechanical presses that ran at a very high speed. When we wanted to start making steel pressure cookers, we had a problem, as stainless steel cookers use hydraulic presses, which ran at a slower speed than the mechanical press. We reviewed the design and technical process and were able to make a breakthrough innovation that allowed us to make stainless steel products in a mechanical press. Stainless steel cannot withstand the force of the speed at which the mechanical press operates and is liable to tear. To explain this engineering complexity in fairly simple terms, our chief manufacturing officer, Rajan, converted the mechanical press functions using servomotors and had them operating like hydraulic presses. I had told Rajan that it was not possible to do so, but he showed that it very much was.

We are the first company in India, and perhaps in the world, to produce stainless steel pressure cookers in a mechanical press.

Anodized cookware

We are the first and only company in India to make hard-anodized cookware, at our plant in Gujarat.

Aluminium cookers are by far the biggest revenue earners, given their cost advantage in our country. Aluminium is an excellent conductor of heat and is cheaper than steel. It is, however, softer, and is damaged by hard use and contact with other metal utensils. It also reacts to hard water.

Hard anodization is an electrochemical process by which the aluminium gets an oxide layer. The protective coat of 60–70 microns gives the vessel resistance to wear, corrosion and temperature, and makes it harder, sturdier and durable, while retaining its quality of heat conductivity. It also makes the aluminium non-reactive with acidic foods.

Hard anodizing makes aluminium stronger than steel, and hard-anodized cookware is also stick-resistant, though not as much as non-stick-coated steel. With these value additions, hard-anodized aluminium costs 50 per cent more than regular aluminium.

Such cookers and cookware are very popular, and we make many models in many different, attractive colours. Our hard-anodized cookware is doing well both in the Indian markets and in exports to OEMs (original equipment manufacturers).

We use the process now for most of our products in the 'cook and serve' category, including the latest clip-on pressure cooker. We call it 'pressure cookware', and it saves one the hassle of using more than one vessel for a dish. You can cook in this pressure cooker, exchange the lid for a glass lid and place it straightaway on the dining table.

We designed this cookware, and we are the sole manufacturers of this product, as nobody else has got the manufacturing facility to make such cookware. It is a very capital-intensive project; it also requires a lot of electricity and economies of scale that comes with high demand leading to volumes for mass manufacturing. We had the resources to invest; we chose a location that has a high supply of power; and we also have the market, making us unique in the industry.

Automation

In Coimbatore and Karjan all the press operations are done by robots. We also use robots for polishing, and will soon automate the assembly too.

We use robots for tasks that need a 360-degree axis, and we use server-controlled special-purpose machines for those jobs that require just a linear plane. The automation industry is also addressing the various needs of companies like ours and are designing two-dimensional and cheaper robots for different applications.

Automation increases safety as well as efficiency. Not too long ago, a factory worker who had spent enough years on the machines would often be missing a finger or two. He would, in fact, view it as a certificate of his experience, and hold up his hand with a missing finger almost as a badge of honour. Automation has ensured better safety for the factory employees.

Making across India

I am the chief engineer of the company. I am a mechanic, a process engineer and a product engineer, all in one. I headed

the team that set up all the new factories and every single process
in the factories at our company (apart from the very first factory
in Bangalore, which we closed in 1991).

With new frontiers opening up in engineering and
manufacturing, we put together an excellent professional team.
Geared up for new challenges, it is headed by H.T. Rajan, our
chief manufacturing officer. He used to head our condom
business, and it was Ravichandran who recommended that we get
him to implement Prestige's factory expansion and new plants.

Ravichandran says, 'I suggested Rajan's name since he has
a futuristic approach that would be of great help as we moved
from a known technology to newer technology.'

We have eight manufacturing units in all across five factories
in the east, west and south of India. The fact that our factories
are located across India is partly by design and partly due to
circumstances, but it reinforces our pan-India presence.

Tamil Nadu (Hosur and Coimbatore)

Our first factory was in Bangalore. We had set up the next
plant in Hosur in neighbouring Tamil Nadu in 1981 to meet
the growing demand for our cookers. In 1991, our Bangalore
factory, which used to be on the outskirts of the city, found
itself in the midst of a residential area as the city had grown by
leaps and bounds around it. We shut down the factory here and
shifted the plant to Coimbatore.

We already had prime land in this major city in Tamil
Nadu. Along with the plant machinery, we also relocated
the people who were working the machines to Coimbatore.
The products that we make in Coimbatore and Hosur cater

largely to the markets in the south and the west. One of our factory units in Hosur won the President's Design Award in 1994.

Uttarakhand (Roorkee)

We took a very big step in 2006 when we stepped outside the south for the first time to set up our third factory in Roorkee to make inner-lid cookers for the market in the north. For years, Ravichandran had been pushing us to start making inner-lid cookers, and when we finally decided on it he pushed for a factory that would be closer to the market. I was not quite sure how we would manage a factory that was 2000 km away, but the team was confident that we would learn how to. We couldn't make the inner-lid product in the south and sell it in the north; we had to make it in the north.

Gujarat (Karjan)

We also set up a fourth factory, a highly power-intensive greenfield project in Karjan to manufacture hard-anodized cookers and non-stick cookware. We chose to set it up in Gujarat, as it was the only state where we could get constant and unlimited electricity.

Until 2011–12, we used to import some quantities of hard-anodized cookware from China and sell them in India. With a growing market for these products, we decided that we should start manufacturing them in India, and were on the lookout for a suitable location where we would get the amount of electricity that the manufacturing plant needed.

Narendra Modi was then the chief minister of Gujarat, and he invited us to set up a plant in that state. He offered to give us uninterrupted supply of power on the condition that we did not install a generator. We bought Bialetti's non-stick cookware unit in Coccaglio, Italy, and installed it in our plant here. Our factory here is a state-of-the-art one and we use robots extensively in the manufacturing processes. It is also our biggest factory.

Maharashtra (Khardi)

Our fifth factory is in Khardi, near Nasik. This was earlier the site of Triveni Bialetti Industries, the Indian unit of the Italian firm, Bialetti.

We wanted to quickly expand the cookware business, and as we had run out of capacities, we were looking to acquire a new plant. We negotiated the takeover for a year. It is a fantastic factory with great machinery and good technology. The products we make here supply all our markets.

We are focusing a lot on exports now. While, at the end of the day, one might say it is only a pot and a pan that we are making, their shape, design and handles are all fashioned to meet different aesthetics. We constantly come up with makeovers to keep our products appealing. Our focus on exports is very intense now, and we offer different designs for different geographies in the export market.

Global standards

Rajan says, 'We have embarked on a digital journey and we have a road map to make all our machines smart. We have a high level of data analytics to improve efficiencies, including energy efficiency. We constantly strive to address the 3 Rs—Reduce, Recycle, Reuse—to reach zero discharge. We use a lot of renewable energy through solar and wind. Our Roorkee factory has been awarded for its use of concentrated solar reflectors. We have a 100-kilowatt solar power plant in Coimbatore.

'The factories have all the statutory and regulatory compliances, and we are on par with all global standards in terms of compliances. We are ISO 9000–compliant in all our factories and are moving towards ISO 14001 and ISO 18001 (environmental and occupational safety standards).

'Our social compliances are high and we are excellent paymasters. We have various categories of workers in our factories, ranging from unskilled, skilled and semi-skilled to highly skilled, who can programme the robots and make the machines smart.'

A matter of equal pride and satisfaction to me is that our factories employ 1500 workers drawn from different parts of the country. They make for a wonderful synthesis of culture. Our Coimbatore factory, for example, has the highest productivity. We employ close to 400 people here, and almost 40 per cent of them are from the northern and eastern parts of India. Over time, the men have married local women, speak the local language and have taken to the local food and customs.

12

MARKETING LOVE

Create a story for your brand that is memorable, and repeat it.

'*Jo biwi se karey pyaar, woh Prestige se kaise karey inkaar?*' When Abhishek Bachchan cooks a delicious meal and serves it to his lovely wife, Aishwarya—using Prestige cookers and cookware, of course—everybody goes 'ooh'. Everybody knows Prestige because of this timeless line celebrating a husband's love for his wife.

Our ads are everywhere—on TV, in print and online. We are among the largest spenders on advertising and marketing in the industry. Close to 6.5 per cent of our costs are marketing and advertising spends, and this has been a consistent investment over the last fifteen years. Our business has grown multifold, and the ad spends have grown in proportion.

Reluctant advertiser

I must admit, though, that I was initially reluctant to advertise. My initial opinion was that it was a waste of money, as I felt everybody knew the brand and there was no need to advertise Prestige. I actually cut advertising expenses when I took over the running of Prestige. But I learnt the hard way that we need to advertise. Our competitor, Hawkins, was advertising extensively in the press, and we were losing market share to it. After I realized that marketing was the name of the game, I was determined to understand it and pick up the tricks of the trade.

Group marketing office

After I had got the Prestige factory functioning smoothly and brought the workers and staff in sync with my vision, my presence was not needed there all the time. I moved to the city in 1979, to a building that had earlier belonged to the Raja of Ramnad. It was used as a godown, where TTK & Company stored the goods it distributed. The building was actually a small palace. The godown and offices were on the lower levels, and there was a suite of rooms upstairs, which was used a guest house. We used to stay in these rooms when we visited Bangalore for vacations. In those days we needed blankets even in May. It's hard to believe that now, as climate change has made the city much warmer. We made this building the Group's marketing office.

I had become the managing director of TTK Group in 1978 and began looking after the marketing of not only Prestige, but also of Durex, Woodward's, Kiwi and other products.

I am not involved in marketing and advertising campaigns these days, but in the beginning I was closely involved in their every aspect. Advertising has been a main ingredient

in our recipe for success, and we have employed some of the
best agencies to produce some timeless ads, working with
advertising personalities like Prahlad Kakkar. We have
worked with different agencies, including HTA, RK Swamy,
MAA and Mudra.

Naughty ads

We came out with many beautiful campaigns, and some naughty
ones too. There was a lot of creativity in advertising those days
and we had fun making our ads, though we were losing money.
When we launched a brand of condom called Fiesta (this was
through our joint venture with the London Rubber Company),
we ran a bold campaign with five-page ads in all the major
magazines. These were coloured condoms and the first of their
kind in the market. Our campaign said, 'If it's Monday, let it be
red,' and so on, for all the days of the week.

India Today, one of the national magazines in which we ran
the ads, came out with a story headlined, 'Contraceptives: Sexy
Shades'. It went on to say, 'The sex life of adult Indians now
seems definitely beyond the pale—ever since the advent of multi-
coloured luxury condoms.' It talked about one of the blurbs in
the ad, which said 'the miracle of the sheath' made young girls'
'cold hauteur' melt in seconds. The ad led to a question being
raised in Parliament.[1]

We had launched a pink condom, Kohinoor, in 1979. In
November 1983, we followed it up with all-colour condoms,

---

[1]   Radhakrishnan, M G. 'Under Control.' India Today, 14 August
       2008. indiatoday.intoday.in/story/Under+control/1/2723.html

Fiesta. Our aggressive sales campaign was followed by a massive capacity expansion programme.

Connecting generations

Another iconic campaign was the one we created for Woodward's. It shows a baby crying and the grandmother advising the young mother to give it Woodward's Gripe Water because that was what she, the grandmother, had given her daughter. The storyline then extended back to the previous generation, the grandmother now asking the great-grandmother what she had given her as a baby. The great-grandma too says she gave her Woodward's Gripe Water. The campaign emphasized that Woodward's was trusted by generations of Indian mothers. It fetched a terrific response.

Showcasing safety

When I invented the GRS, I knew this enhanced safety aspect of our cookers would be a game changer, and I wanted an ad campaign that would project it. We had to show people that Prestige pressure cookers were the safest. We had to regain the clients we had lost, and quickly get new customers. Everything hinged on the advertising campaign, but our agency at the time did not seem to be in sync with what we needed.

We looked around for another agency, and after a market evaluation our team suggested that we go with MAA Communications. I asked Bunty and Sadiqa Peerbhoy, who headed MAA in Bangalore, to take it up.

Bunty had been, in fact, my first friend in Bangalore. Our fathers were friends, and when I moved here Bunty too was a newcomer to the city. We were both interested in horse racing and spent the weekends at the races. We developed a good friendship, and through him I met many people, some of whom have become great friends. Our families got along very well too, and when the kids were younger we used to go on family vacations together.

Our company had done business with MAA's head office in Bombay in the past, but for some years the TTK account was with other agencies. When our team suggested that MAA was the agency best suited to take up the task of creating an ad for the GRS, Latha and I went over to their place for a drink. That evening, I asked them to take charge of advertising for Prestige. The year was 1980.

Jo biwi se karey pyaar

Sadiqa Peerbhoy had earlier written the classic line 'Timekeepers to the nation', for HMT, and she wrote this seemingly simple copy that has become one of the most iconic lines in Indian advertising: *'Jo biwi se karey pyaar, woh Prestige se kaise karey inkaar?'* (How can a man who loves his wife say no to Prestige?). This line has since been played around with time and again in many situations in the country. While it was used as a meme during Prime Minister Modi's election campaign, *'Jo desh se karey pyaar, woh Modi se kaise karey inkaar?'* (How can anyone who loves their country, say no to Modi?), cricket legend Virender Sehwag tweeted a selfie with his wife with the caption, '*Jo biwi se kare pyaar, woh selfie se kaise kare inkaar?*'[2]

Sadiqa explains the ad, 'The campaign had to show that Prestige was the safest pressure cooker, and this claim would cast an aspersion on the safety of other cooker brands. We did not want to get into a headlong conflict with them as we felt that that wouldn't be nice. We decided to wrap this up in emotion and make it an expression of a husband's love. In those days, in middle-class homes, the husband and wife went together to buy a pressure cooker.

'The first commercial was about a husband and wife shopping for a pressure cooker. The husband asks the shopkeeper to show him a pressure cooker: "Pressure cooker *dikhayega* . . ." and the shopkeeper starts saying, "If you want an ordinary pressure cooker, I can show you this . . . or if you want something else, I can show you this . . . But, if you love your wife, then you would want to buy the safest cooker." The husband intends to buy the cheapest cooker, but he is with his wife at the store. He glances at her and says, "Give me Prestige," which is the most expensive cooker.'

'The campaign specifically addressed the question of safety and allayed fears of the Prestige cooker bursting and causing

2   IREF—Indian Real Estate Forum, https://api.indianrealestateforum. com/api//v0/at t a chment s/f e t ch-a t t a chme n t ?node_ id=2230099&type=attach; IndianRealEstateForum.com. 'Narendra Modi Indian Prime Minister | IREF—Indian Real Estate Forum', www.indianrealestateforum.com/forum/iref%C2%AE-lounge/the-off-topic-forum/indianpolitics/bjp/63718-narendra-modi--indian-prime-minister/page121?p=1577163; Zee News Hindi, Zee News, 29 July 2017, zeenews.india.com/hindi/sports/cricket/virendra-sehwag-shared-a-pic-with-hiswife-on-twitter-saying/334700.

physical damage,' explains Bunty. 'It was a beautiful way of dealing with the resistance to its price. Here we justified the purchase of a more expensive cooker because the husband was looking out for the safety of his wife. And there's no price on love.'

Early TV adopter

In the eighties, television was fairly new and people were not comfortable with it. Nobody believed that television was going to be a huge advertising medium. Bunty pushed for television because we needed to demonstrate the GRS, and he felt that nothing could do this better than an audio-visual medium. Bunty says, 'The TV ad campaign we released for Prestige was once again a game changer for the company. Those were the early days of television in India, and we ran the ad on Doordarshan (the state-owned and the only TV channel in those years), and got a lot of mileage out of that. That helped the fortunes of Prestige, as sales took off immediately.

'We worked on equally popular follow-ups to this campaign. One of the films had a man going home with a Prestige cooker strapped to his bike, and all along the way people look and him to say, "Woh tho biwi se pyaar karta hai (He loves his wife)".'

The postman's angry knock

Another ad we made for the launch of the pressure pan ended up upsetting the Postmen's Association of India! We wanted to show that the pressure pan was a very versatile vessel—that you can fry, sauté, cook and steam and do many things in it, apart from pressure cooking. The ad commercial showed a woman throwing out all her old kadais and pans, one of which lands on a postman. While all of us agreed with the agency that it was a funny ad, it got us a legal notice from the Postmen's Association as they felt we had made the postman look foolish. The ad was a major success though, and the Prestige pressure pan became a huge hit.

Change of line

In 2001 we dropped one of my favourite lines from our ad campaign for Prestige, *'Jo biwi se . . .'*

Chandru Kalro, who was then head of marketing, says, 'We had decided to move beyond pressure cookers and cookware, and into gas stoves and appliances. After a major consumer survey we had created an entire product range that was different from our competition's. This was the time when open kitchens were becoming common and customers wanted products that were distinctly superior. The original line *"jo biwi se karey pyaar"* was based on the safety platform. We had moved beyond safety and our campaign had to be relevant.

'So a new campaign with the tagline "Are you ready for a smarter kitchen?" was launched along with the new product lines. The whole idea was to position Prestige as a better and smarter alternative, based on its innovation across its product lines. This was very successful. We launched several new categories of products over the next twelve years, and we positioned ourselves as a "total kitchen solutions" company.'

Love returns

But much to my satisfaction, a few years later, everybody in the company felt the old line would work again, albeit with a tweak.

'After a very successful stint with the "smarter kitchen" tagline, we conducted another major consumer survey on our brand, in 2014, on what people thought of the brand and its attributes,' says Kalro. 'We found that while customers agreed that we were innovative, there was a need to go beyond rational points, like differentiation, to make a bigger and more lasting connect with the consumer. We also found that the old line of "*Jo biwi se . . .*" had an unaided recall of 100 per cent. This, along with the fact that men were also now participating in the affairs of the kitchen and cooking, prompted a rethink.

'We came up with the idea of bringing back the old line in a new context—of the man participating in the cooking and thereby expressing his love for his wife. The emotional quotient of this thought was very high, and we decided that this huge decision needed a celebrity couple to make the impact much larger.

'We needed a pan-India connect, and we found that actor Aishwarya, who had this connect, and her husband, Abhishek, who had a fun personality, would be the ideal choice. They were also non-controversial, which was very important to us. The new campaign was thus born. It had three themes—fun, food and togetherness.

'So it was that in 2014 we reprised the line iconic line, "*Jo biwi se karey pyaar, woh Prestige se kaise karey inkaar?*", giving it a different slant, again, in keeping with the times. The campaign showed a loving husband cooking for his wife. Instead of buying a pressure cooker for his wife, he was using it himself. The new-age twist in this ad campaign was a huge hit. The extensive shooting sessions were fun for the whole team, including when Abhishek Bachchan came up with this line on the sets: "*Meri biwi pe seeti mat bajaana* (don't whistle at my wife)."

'The campaign featuring the Bollywood power couple premiumized the Prestige brand. The campaign was a huge hit, making us the brand leader.'

Evolving with time

Advertising and marketing is very important. Our former marketing director at TTK Prestige, Nowroji, explains how it has evolved in our company:

'When pressure cookers were launched in India, it was a new market. We had to move people from cooking in pots to cooking in pressure cookers. They needed a lot of reassurance, especially regarding pressure cookers as, if they are not used properly, they can be dangerous. Advertising communication plays a key role in making people understand the importance of maintenance, of replacing worn out gaskets, etc. Our communication helped people recognize concepts such as shelf life, gasket, safety valve and other such matters. It also reassured them that they were buying a premium product because of its safety and certification.

'We began to run integrated service and exchange campaigns, apart from free service campaigns every six months. At one time, all our 400 dealers in Chennai ran the campaign simultaneously. This was part of a uniform strategy for several years and became integral to our campaigns.

'These campaign communications serve two purposes; they build brand awareness, and they help us remove old cookers from the market, minimizing problems later. We scrapped worn-out cookers and offered discounts on new purchases.

'With the plethora of appliances we were offering, there was a need to create a branding story that was differentiated from those of conventional kitchen utensils. This story would have to add value in the minds of the consumer.

'Continuous advertising sends subliminal messages; and not just when a launch happens. The branding story provides continuous awareness and, over a period of time, people start recognizing the brand. There is a taken-for-granted factor too, especially when products have a long life cycle, as in the case of pressure cookers.

'Continuous communication also offers reassurance about your product so that when the customer wants to replace an existing product or add a second product, he or she would again buy a Prestige.

'An umbrella communication builds reassurance in an established market. Each time we launch a new product we back it up with advertising. It's still the most effective medium for us. Over the years, we have, of course, evolved from just vanilla mass media advertising to digital marketing, alongside consumer contact programmes like service camps and exchange programmes.'

13

SKORE AND MORE

'The ballpark keeps changing, and
we need to play accordingly'—T.T. Raghunathan

From dawn to dusk, you could choose from the TTK Group's vast portfolio of products to suit almost every need of yours: deodorants, snacks, cookers, condoms, pharmaceuticals, medical devices and much more.

My younger brother, T.T. Raghunathan, is the executive chairman of TTK Healthcare. Established in 1958 as Orient Pharma Pvt. Ltd, it was renamed TTK Healthcare in 1999, and has been a publicly listed company since 1985. TTK Healthcare operates through four strategic business units (SBUs): pharmaceuticals, consumer products, biomedical devices and foods. The Group's condom business, TTK Protective Devices Ltd, was merged with the healthcare company in December 2017.

This chapter is *Raghu's* story of creating new brands, such as Skore condoms and Eva personal care products, and the company's renewed focus on some key businesses like food and medical devices.

Break from the past

The Group took a radical decision in 2003 that meant giving up a legacy of business, and this came about as a result of painful learnings over a period of time. From condoms to toiletries, the TTK Group was the first to start selling some of the world's most famous brands in India, starting from 1928. However, over the last several years, it has been distributing only the brands it owns.

K. Shankaran, group director (corporate affairs), TTK Group, explains the sequence of events leading up to this marked shift in the Group's business: 'Alongside our home-grown brands and those that we had bought (Prestige and Woodward's Gripe Water), we had continued the original business of selling third-party brands using our immense distribution network. This involved considerable investment and efforts in building those brands.

'Over the course of time, though, our efforts did not always benefit us. For example, TTK Prestige had marketed Braun's epilators (then owned by Gillette). But when Braun was acquired by P&G, the relationship ended, and all the work that we had put into establishing the brand in India paid off for P&G, leaving us with the short end of the stick. That was when TTK Prestige decided to end third-party brand distribution deals.

'TTK Healthcare continued to market several third-party brands, such as Brylcreem (men's haircare) and Kiwi (shoe polish) for Sara Lee and Dr Scholls for SSL. We also launched 3M's

Scotch-Brite in India. With periodic renewal of agreements, though, the margins were shrinking. The constant change of ownership of the brands outside India further compounded the problems.'

Losing Kohinoor

Shankaran explains how the company came to lose its prized condom brands. 'Our biggest blow was in the condom business when we lost our crown jewel, Kohinoor condoms. The TTK Group introduced condoms in India, way back in 1948. This was a bold move by T.T. Narasimhan.

'The very first condom that we brought here was Durapac (later known as Durex), under a distribution arrangement with London Rubber Company (LRC). The Group had started LRC India, a joint venture between TTK and LRC, UK. The JV was renamed TTK LIG when LRC changed its name to London International Group. TTK LIG was the first of the Group companies to be publicly listed in 1974. (It was delisted later.)

'We created a new condom brand, Kohinoor, in India in 1979. It became a top seller (see Chapter 12: Marketing Love). The premium global brand, Durex, was rolled out in India in 1997, and we manufactured Durex for the local and export markets. TTK Healthcare marketed Kohinoor and Durex in India, while LIG handled exports and marketing for Durex worldwide. We supplied 40 per cent of Durex's worldwide demand.

'The JV continued without a hiccup even after LIG was acquired by SSL International Plc in 1999. In 2010, when Reckitt Benckiser acquired SSL International, Reckitt became TTK's joint venture partner here by virtue of that purchase.

'After Reckitt entered the picture, we felt that it was seeking to unilaterally change the agreement with us to its benefit, at the cost of the joint venture. The matter also went to court. In the end, we bought out Reckitt's 49.8 per cent stake and the entire manufacturing unit. As we had contributed technology to the company, we also retained the technology. But Reckitt took away our prized Kohinoor brand from us. The bitter loss seemed like a sad repeat of the British taking the Kohinoor diamond from India.

'The Kohinoor episode reinforced our decision to focus on our core businesses. We decided to promote only our own products, and even as we decided to stop distributing products of other brands, we realized that we needed to fill the gap with our own consumer products.'

Skore

After the split, Reckitt Benckiser took both Kohinoor and Durex brands, and we bought the factories that belonged to the TTK LIG JV. We set up TTK Protective Devices Ltd with the factories, which had the capacity to produce 2.1 billion condoms. We had the technology, we had state-of-the-art machinery, and we had the resources. We had everything but a product and a brand. Almost overnight, we had nothing to manufacture.

We were not going give up, though. As pioneers of condom manufacturing in India, and having been in the business for over fifty years, we knew the channels and had a great understanding of distribution. All the key people in our condom business, including the CEO and the marketing manager, had quit, except a young brand manager, Vishal Vyas. I built a new brand with just Vyas to help me. He is now the marketing manager, and I would attribute a big part of our success to him.

Enhancing pleasure

It was important to getting the brand name right, and we went through a lot of iterations. Our advertising agency, McCann, worked very hard, and we came up with 'Skore'. The brand imagery we created around it was very different from what we had had for Kohinoor, which was advertised as a married couple's family planning aid.

We positioned Skore as a pre-marital pleasure enhancer, and it clicked. It went on to be named among the ten most successful launches in Nielsen's 2016 evaluation of 16,000 brand launches in India.

Aggressive campaign

Vishal Vyas, general manager, marketing, recalls the campaign: 'Even while the protracted negotiations were going on, we were prepared for the worst and determined to face the challenge. On 8 November 2012, the same day the split was formally announced, we launched the Skore brand. It was a glitzy launch with the theme "Don't just play the game of love. Skore." The same morning we had a front-page ad in the leading newspapers. We were very aggressive, not just for commercial reasons, but for emotional reasons too.

'We didn't compromise on quality. We had a good product as we had the production capacity, and our sales experience in retail helped us a lot. We knew who sold condoms and how they sold condoms. These two factors helped us achieve a 10 per cent market share in just three years of our launch. (Manforce, Mankind Pharma—30 per cent, Moods, HLL Lifecare—12 per cent, Skore, TTK—10 per cent.) We overtook older brands like Kohinoor and Kamasutra, and that was a victory we relished.'

Youth-centric

'While our rapport with retailers could help us in the beginning, as they can place our product, that would not guarantee continued business unless we attracted customers,' Vyas explains. 'We decided to make ours a youth brand as that was where we found a gap. We wanted to do things that were different from what the existing players were doing and establish Skore as a fun and friendly product for the youth.

'In our bid to be different, we held India's first condom fashion show, where all the clothes were made of condoms. We held 'Skore Fashionista' in January 2014, and it was quite an eye-opener, emphasizing that condoms were fashionable.

'We approached fashion design institutes in Mumbai to participate in the contest and the show. Initially, there was reluctance from the professors, who were not sure if their students, most of whom were female, would be comfortable taking it up. They were also anxious about how the students' families would respond. But the young students came out with good ideas and made very interesting clothes out of condoms.'

Cutting through the clutter

There were more disruptive actions on our part, as Vyas points out enthusiastically: 'We aimed at disruption on all fronts. Even our advertising was very different. We created a video series centred on a character called Dr S, who offers fun and quirky tips. We came up with quirky merchandise, such as the condom bookcase. We found that keeping condoms at home was a problem for most young people. So we came up with a naughty idea, making a case for condoms that looks like book.

'Condom disposal was another issue we addressed. We offer elegant and plain waterproof disposal pouches. We also launched two new variants of the condom: Quick Skore, a disposable condom pack that, as its name indicates, can be opened very quickly, and the Champion range of advanced condoms which we launched with Gayle & Dwayne Bravo, which includes India's thinnest condom, and climax-delaying, dotted and ribbed condoms. We have customized the lyrics of Bravo's "Champion" song for the product. We also have flavoured condoms, cool condoms and warm condoms.

'Some might like our advertisements and some might not, but everyone notices them as we introduce new ads each year. For example, we launched the tagline "Leave the real chocolate for good boys" for our chocolate-flavoured condoms. Women love dots, and so we released dotted condoms.

'We also priced Skore lower to attract the youth, though it is of the same high quality as Durex. Breaking through the clutter helped us reach the number three position in just three years' time. We have a strong urban presence throughout India.

'Quality products, innovative ideas and disruptive advertising have helped us gain recognition as a young and innovative brand. We won Brand Equity's innovative brand award in the condoms category in 2015 and the Silver in the APPIES (Asia Pacific award) for marketing effectiveness.'

The Skore brand is going to move from sexual wellness to pleasure. We have already launched lubricants, and deodorants are next. We also have plans to launch products in a category that is several times the size of the condom market, but we can't talk about it now except to say that it is happening in 2018. We are investing a lot in this brand and will wake up a sleepy category.

Emphasis on quality

I am particular that quality is not about making 100 condoms, applying quality standards and throwing out thirty condoms. It is about making the perfect condom to start with. This is implicit in our operations. R. Sharanyan, executive director, operations, proudly says: 'Any condom factory in the world is led by a person who has trained at TTK's condom factory. Condom factories are located primarily in south-east Asia, with Thailand, Malaysia being the major producers. India is also a major producer. And TTK is a pioneer in this business.'

Even after our split with Reckitt Benckiser, we continue to make Durex condoms for them. They know that we have the highest quality standards and asked us to take it up as contract manufacturer. We agreed to do so, as, if we didn't make them, someone else would.

'The first condom factory in India was the one our Group set up in 1963, in Pallavaram, Chennai, as LRC India. Selling condoms was slow going initially, as the government's position was that India's large population was an asset and that we didn't need population control. In 1968, my uncle, T.T. Vasu, got a grant from Sweden to make condoms, and presented 80 million condoms free to the government to start its family-planning programme. We went on to supply the Nirodh brand of condoms at a subsidized price to the government for some years.

Since then, our Group had consistently invested in factories, and from making 30 million pieces per annum in 1963, we had moved up to 2.1 billion pieces a year. We had three factories. We closed down the oldest of them in Chennai in 2015, and we now have one in Virudhunagar in Tamil Nadu and one in Puducherry, with a combined capacity of 900 million pieces a year.

Innovating machinery

'Nearly all the machines that make condoms are fabricated in-house, in the factories. When we were commissioning the plant in Puducherry, we made all the machines there,' Sharanyan says with pride.

'We have created a hybrid between the older mini-plants in Asia that are slower and need a lot of manpower, and the fully automated European plants, which consume a lot of power. We merged both to fabricate the "midi-plant" or the medium automated plant. Combining the efficiency of a fully automated machine with the energy-saving feature of a mini-plant was an innovation by the project team in Puducherry. This enables us to produce high volumes at a lower cost.'

Our factories help the local economy. Virudhunagar, near Madurai, was a village when our factory was set up. My father, T.T. Narasimhan, decided to set up a facility here as my grandfather, T.T. Krishnamachari, was very close to the legendary politician of Tamil Nadu, Kamarajar, who was born in Virudhunagar. It has grown into a prosperous town because of the TTK Group.

Not tonight, love

Durex's feud with TTK was alarming news in the UK as TTK made more than half of the popular Durex condoms that were imported by Britain. The *Daily Mail* reported this on 25 July 2011:

> Not tonight, love . . . Health fears as Britain hit by condom shortage
>
> *Britain is facing a shortage of condoms following a dispute between leading brand Durex and its key supplier.*
>
> The news has sparked fears of an increase in sexually transmitted diseases and unwanted pregnancies, as the NHS issued a statement warning of 'disruption' to the supply.
>
> Sexual health expert Dr. Malcolm Vandenburg said the shortage could put the safe sex message at risk, saying: 'The fear is that if there is a shortage, young people will begin to have unprotected sex.
>
> 'Once they get used to doing this, they may continue not to use condoms even when the supply is back to normal.'

> The Slough-based company launched a High
> Court bid to force TTK to resume supply, but the
> claim was rejected.
>
> A spokesman said the company was 'actively
> managing the situation to mitigate any damage'.
>
> Durex is Britain's most popular brand of condom,
> accounting for 40 per cent of the market. TTK makes
> more than half of them.

Eva

Just as the success of Skore proves that it is not necessarily one's
size or clout that will lead to success, so does our achievement
in making Eva the number one deodorant for women in the
country. My grandfather started life as a distributor of Lever's,
so consumer products would always be our focus.

Sara Lee TTK was our joint venture with Sara Lee Corp
of America, established in 1992–93, and it manufactured
Kiwi shoe polish and Brylcreem (haircare product for men);
these were distributed by TTK Healthcare. In 2001–02,
however, Sara Lee decided to exit the JV with us and took the
business to Godrej Consumer Products Ltd. We had taken
their fuddy-duddy products, Kiwi and Brylcreem, and made
them fashionable. Their exit meant the loss of a business worth
Rs 100 crore for us. We had also sold Dr Scholl's footwear
business to Reckitt Benckiser when we parted ways.

We needed new brands to sell, and to replace the brands
that we had lost. In 2002–03, we launched a cosmetic brand
called Eva that we had bought from Sara Lee a couple of years

earlier. It is aimed at teenagers and has become hugely popular as a skin-friendly product. It is the first brand without alcohol and is pH-balanced.

We paid Rs 50 lakh for the brand, and we have grown the business to a turnover of Rs 90 crore. It is the leading Indian brand of deodorants for women.

Eva is a young girl's affordable cosmetic; it offers superior quality at a quarter of the price. We are scaling up the business, and we have a range of eye, nail, lip and skincare cosmetics, then talc and more, apart from deodorants.

Good Home

We also launched another brand called Good Home in 2007, which is a range of cleaning products, including scrubbers, air fresheners, room fresheners, odour removers, drain cleaners, and vegetable and fruit wash.

Food: Turning up the heat

From contemplating selling the company's foods division for a mere Rs 3–4 crore to ramping up investment in it, I came full circle. This happened when I realized that the company's innovative product Fryums had become generic, even finding mention in the sales tax schedule as 'Fryums-type products'.

My brother had introduced the ready-to-eat snacks in this country in 1990 by getting Italian machines to make ready-to-fry extruded-potato-and-cereal-based snack pellets, or papads, of great quality and in hygienic conditions. (See Chapter 10A: Cooking Up Inventions.)

An even greater reason to stay on in foods was the size of the market. While the ready-to-fry snack pellets market is about Rs 2000 crore and consists of both organized and unorganized manufacturers, TTK Foods operates in the upper end of the price spectrum (upwards of Rs 50 per kg), where the market narrows down to about Rs 500 crore.

We are giving great attention to the foods business now, and apart from adding new production lines in our old factory in Hoskote, near Bengaluru, to make 800 tonnes a year in 2010, we also set up a new factory in Jaipur to produce 1000 tonnes of the snacks in 2016. There is a long-term geographical advantage in having a factory in Jaipur. As the raw material comes from there and the market is there too, the investment will pay off eventually.

Fryums are available in varying bases: potato, cereal, rice, pulses and corn, and, more recently, hummus and quinoa, the latter of which used to be sourced from Peru earlier but is now grown in India. Fryums come in thirty different shapes, including 2D wheels, sticks, stars, checks, ribbed chips, etc., and 3D triangles, hearts, pillows, and in a whole lot of flavours, including onion, garlic, coriander and mint.

Pani puri

An earlier innovation of ours was the pani puri pellet, which is a hygienic way to get this all-time favourite Indian street food. My nephew, Lakshman Thattai, who was heading the foods division when the pellet was launched, says, 'Pani puris are typically manufactured in unhygienic surroundings. Our compressed pani puri pellet just needs to be dropped into hot oil and it becomes a puri, the Fryum 3D! We are the biggest manufacturers of pani puri in India by far, and have one-third of the market.'

B2B challenge

Ranganath Rao, senior vice president at the Group, is a TTK veteran who has been handling the foods business for the last couple of years. He says the company's greatest advantage is that 'it is probably the only professionally run company in the industry, as most of the others are owned by small-time business people. While there are challenges in depending on B2B distribution, the company's infrastructure, operational and capacity strengths are major advantages'.

R&D for innovation

Talking about the strengths of the company, Rao says, 'We are the only company in the industry to have a full-fledged R&D centre, a product team and a pilot plant. They are located in Bengaluru. This has enabled us to reach out beyond its primary customers of wholesalers and repackagers to cover the entire spectrum of the market.

'The pilot plant allows clients to see the final product for themselves, and this is our greatest strength. The R&D team enables us to work with any large company, like PepsiCo India, and helps us develop new, customized products.

'Our ability to constantly innovate has led to the growth of exports into a major vertical. We export to a dozen countries directly and to another half a dozen indirectly. Our products are present in about eighteen countries. We export directly to countries in Asia, east Asia, south-east Asia and Canada, and indirectly to south Asia, Malaysia and Singapore. Apart from PepsiCo India, PepsiCo in South Africa, Saudi Arabia and Iraq are also our customers.'

Global trends

Snacking is a big global habit, and people want variety. The snacking habits vary, of course, from region to region. For example, in south India, snacks are mainly an accompaniment to food, and the preference is for less spicy snacks. In north India, snacks are to be had with drinks, and they like them spicier.

Tastes differ across the world. The Middle East is the largest snacking market; there people prefer cereal-based snacks. In Europe there is a fondness for potato-based snacks, and a little bit for cereal and corn snacks too. Australians and south east Asians like potato and cereal-based snacks. The US is also a very big snacking market for potato and corn-based snacks. We haven't exported to the US as yet.

Tripling turnover

Typically, Fryums and pani puri pellets are sold to wholesalers, who repackage them under various names and sell them. Consumers do not know that it is from the house of TTK, though in a few multiplexes we sell Fryums ourselves. We plan to launch brands in the next couple of years, and the foray into B2C from a wholly B2B segment will take the business to the next level. The current turnover from the foods division is Rs 90 crore, less than 10 per cent of Group turnover. The Group is investing considerably in this business, and we aim to triple the turnover to reach Rs 300 crore in five years' time.

Medical Devices

Among our most interesting products are medical devices, such as heart valves and knee replacements, which are vitally needed in the country.

TTK Chitra Heart Valves

TTK Healthcare manufactures and distributes the most affordable heart valve prosthesis in the world. The TTK Chitra Heart Valve is India's first indigenous heart valve, and is regarded as a very significant contribution to healthcare. This critical medical device has helped 1,00,000 patients so far. We are the only company, apart from some firms in the US, that makes such heart valves.

The heart valve was a project initially conceived in 1978 and developed over twelve years at the Sree Chitra Tirunal Institute for Medical Sciences and Technology in Thiruvananthapuram, Kerala. TTK took up the challenge of commercial production of the tilting disc heart valve. It was my father's brainchild. We perfected the manufacturing, working alongside the team from Chitra Tirunal. We received the President's Award for the product's successful commercialization.

Rheumatic heart disease leads to valve damage, and this was very prevalent in India. Consequently, the incidence of heart valve replacement was very high. The Chitra heart valves came as a saviour to people who could have their heart valves replaced at a very affordable cost of Rs 10,000 a valve. Imported valves are much more expensive. One lakh valves made by us beat in the hearts of people, and they are the cheapest anywhere in the world.

Knee and hip replacements

The TTK Ortho division makes total knee replacements in technical collaboration with Dr M.J. Pappas and Dr F.F. Buechel's M/s. BP Trust. Dr Pappas received his PhD from Rutgers University in mechanical engineering, specializing in computer-aided structural design, and is an internationally recognized expert in advanced design. Dr Buechel is a renowned orthopaedic surgeon, researcher and developer in the field of total joint replacement.

These designs are US FDA–approved and are a result of over twenty-five years of development, clinical investigation and use. TTK's Ortho division uses state-of-the-art software for 3D modelling of complicated profiles and for accurate generation of articulating surfaces of knee implants.

We bought a company that was in this business, Invicta Meditek Ltd, in 2009. Our devices are marketed by TTK Healthcare under the brand name Altius. It's just now turning a profit. We have been exporting to Europe too. Prosthetics is a sunrise industry; the concept of knee and hip replacement is becoming more acceptable. We will soon be expanding to hip replacements.

S. Kalyanaraman, director and company secretary, TTK Healthcare, says, 'We have the advantage of being a heterogeneous company with several businesses, and each of these businesses offers good opportunities. We are market leaders in many categories; the Woodward's Gripe Water brand is the market leader in the babycare category, Eva is the number one brand in the women's deodorant category, Skore is number three in just three years' time, and Good Home is also shaping up well.

'The last two decades have seen steady growth for the company. We exited businesses that were not relevant or not growing, such as bulk drugs, printing, paper, hospital disposables, spinning and hosiery. We improved the operative performance and have reached a point where our earnings have gone up to Rs 70–80 crore, and we are a cash-rich company.'

14

BUSINESS NOT AS USUAL

*If an idea does not succeed, you try another and
then another until one succeeds.*

We have incubated many new businesses, some of which have failed and some of which have succeeded. I have enjoyed the process of supporting new entrepreneurs. A couple of them have fascinating stories to tell, and their growth is interestingly intertwined.

One such company started off in the early days of the Internet, when Girish Rao, who was TTK Prestige's vice president of marketing, spoke to me about leaving the company to start his own business. His business idea seemed interesting, and I could see that Girish had a lot of potential and felt he could run the business successfully. The Group invested in the new business, TTK NRI Services, and so did I in a personal capacity.

NRI Services

In those days, young Indians who moved abroad to work used to rely on their friends and extended family to help their ageing parents in India. As this trend was increasing, I saw merit in a business model offering services to such non-resident Indians.

Rao is currently chairman and managing director of Vidal Healthcare Services Pvt. Ltd. He recalls his 'intrapreneurial' experience with TTK:

'It was 1997. Those were very early days of the Internet. In the US, Amazon was just being born. As a vice president of the TTK Group, I travelled frequently, and I was sure that the Internet would really grow and that people would shop on it.

'In 1998–99, there were hints that I was being groomed to become the managing director of TTK Prestige some day. But I wanted to do something on my own and said so to TTJ. He responded by offering to start a new business with me and he incubated it, and that was how TTK NRI Services was born. These days, it's called "intrapreneurial competency building". TTK did that with me way back in 1999–2000, long before business schools started talking about the concept.

'I had already grown very well in the company, which I had joined as a product manager in 1990. I became regional sales manager, then head of the southern region and, within a year of this, TTJ made me the general manager, sales, in 1994. That was a very important phase in my life. I didn't think I was ready for that role but he was very confident about me. I still remember the day he gave me the promotion letter. I had walked out of his office to mine, and minutes later he walked into my cabin with a handwritten note in which he had reflected upon his own affairs in the early days. He had noted the characteristics in me that he liked, what he believed were my strengths and why he thought I was the right guy for the job. It was a three-page handwritten note. It built enormous confidence in me as my predecessor was fifty-five years old and I was just thirty. I still have that letter with me.

'In 1995, I abruptly decided that I must explore life outside the TTK system. The telecom revolution had just happened, and I joined a telecom company in Bombay. I was employee number three at Hutchison Telecom, which later became Vodafone. TTJ was very upset, but I didn't burn my bridges with the Group, and served a very long notice period of four and a half months.

'A couple of years later, for personal reasons, I had to move back to Bangalore, where I was to handle Hutchison's paging operations. When TTJ learnt about it, he wanted me back, and I joined TTK Group as vice president, international. I worked very closely with him during the Manttra days, and in a few years' time I was given the task of handling both international and domestic sales and marketing.'

Failure

Rao recalls, 'With TTJ's backing, I started TTK Services, initially for providing services to NRIs. It didn't take off as expected, and failed, though we struggled to make it work. A couple of years later, we acquired another interesting business, Bharatplanet, which used to provide an innovative service connecting the Internet haves (NRIs) and the Internet have-nots (their parents). The service was called Bharatmail, and was hugely popular as a free service for NRIs. It served nearly half a million users.

'We acquired that company to get access to the NRI population as that was our target audience. We tried for a few years to get it going, but after a while I felt I could be doing something more exciting and proposed yet another new venture.

'At first TTJ almost threw me out, saying, "You just burned Rs 4 crore and now you want more money for another brilliant idea." But luckily for me, he was prepared to give me one more hearing, and we put together a focus group and the leadership team heard me out.

'The idea for this business tied in with the liberalization of the insurance sector in India by the government. Third-party administrators (TPA) were to be licensed to administer health insurance policies, as the newly instituted Insurance Regulatory & Development Authority (IRDA) wanted insurance claims to be processed independent of the insurance companies, to avoid irregularities. I saw the similarities between this and what we were doing for NRIs in TTK Services in offering service care to their parents in India. We had created a structure of hospitals and doctors, which could well be used for the TPA business.'

Healthcare services

Rao explains the new business idea: 'Out of that idea, in 2002, was born the company called TTK Healthcare Services, which was a third-party administrator in the health insurance business. It turned out to be a great business, and we also got private equity (PE) investment. Swiss Re, a Fortune 500 company which is in the reinsurance business globally, acquired it 2006, and TTK and the PE investors got very good returns on the investments they had made.

'As part of that acquisition, I had to work with Swiss Re for a minimum of two years, and I handled their healthcare strategy globally. Having worked with TTK, it was not easy to work for anybody else, and I felt that I would be better off on my own. I quit Swiss Re, and as luck would have it, the company decided to exit the TPA business, and in 2011, I acquired it back from Swiss Re and renamed it Vidal Health TPA. It is now a fairly large TPA in India, and I own it fully. We administer insurance for 75 million lives and employ over 1700 people, mainly in India. We have some business in the Middle East too. My journey as an entrepreneur came about because of TTJ.'

We exited the TPA business when we decided to get into health insurance with Cigna as we could not be in both businesses. (Cigna TTK is a health insurance firm established as a joint venture between the US-based global insurance player Cigna and the TTK Group in 2012. TTK is set to exit the joint venture in 2018.) While Girish had moved on from TTK Services, Sunder P., the co-founder of Bharatplanet, showed remarkable perseverance and, over time, went on to grow the business. It is one of our smallest businesses, and provides a range of services to NRIs (YourManinIndia), concierge services (GetFriday), a housing portal (HomeShikari) and immigration documentation (Immidart).

Some of these businesses didn't succeed, but that didn't stop me from backing new ideas because I'm never one to walk away from business. Had that been the case, I would have given up long ago. If an idea does not succeed, you try another and then another until you succeed. I have backed Sunder in a series of businesses. Sunder is managing director, TTK Services Pvt. Ltd; director, TTK Property Services Pvt. Ltd; and partner, Immidart Technologies LLP.

Sunder narrates the story of his journey with TTK: 'I was a co-founder of Bharatplanet, which was started in 1998. Girish Rao invited us to merge with TTK Services, and I joined the merged entity as the COO in 2002. We got in a few high-profile angel investors from the US.

'The merger was supposed to bring together the benefits of our large user base and the expertise and brand value of the TTK Group. However, that was easier said than done. We were trying to suddenly graduate the freebie-accustomed NRI clients to a premium value-added service in an era when no one was paying anything for online services. Call it an idea that was ahead of its time that could not garner critical mass, or call it bad luck. Think Portea Medical today, think cashless access to insurance, which isn't a big thing today but didn't exist then. We had it all covered, way back in 2003.

'Timing is everything, and we failed on that count. Nevertheless, through this tough period, TTJ always backed us and never talked about shutting down the business.'

Concierge service

'The next critical turning point occurred towards the end of 2003,' says Sunder. 'Girish had already moved on to form the TPA business for the Group. A board meeting was convened to determine if we ought to continue or shut shop. The board agreed to my request for a chance to turn it around and discussed how to pivot the business. They infused more funds for us to take a shot at a new idea: a concierge service in India for NRIs. At that point we were down to five employees in the business, including me. What tipped the decision was TTJ's firm belief that something could be done to make the venture a success. I guess he agreed to it because he was convinced that I believed it could happen.

'From there, it has been a long journey, along which we turned the corner and became profitable in 2007. We later ventured into the unrelated area of virtual assistance for global clients, quite accidentally.

HomeShikari

The next venture was in the real estate marketing space, says Sunder: 'In 2011, I went to TTJ along with his youngest son, Venky (Venkatesh, who worked with me from 2006 to 2014), with an idea for a real estate service that aimed to bring transparency to the opaque real estate market in India. Though TTJ was initially apprehensive, our persistent efforts paid off, and he backed the venture. The business did not take off as anticipated because of the complexities involved. Other competitors, like Housing.com, raised tons of money, but eventually failed to make an impact. We pulled back in time. The venture still exists, but with a different business model that aims to make it the most reliable brokerage and property management company in real estate. You can see the Google reviews of happy customers on the site.'

Immigration services

Never one to say die, after shutting down the HomeShikari venture, Sunder had yet another business proposal. Sunder says, 'While TTJ was quite disappointed that the venture did not pan out as expected, that did not stop me from approaching him again with a business idea in 2014. A couple of people whom I knew from Wipro were planning a start-up in the immigration space. I saw a lot of synergy in what they intended to do and what we were doing as an immigration services provider at TTK. What was solely missing for us was a technology platform that could help us provide a wide range of services at a hugely scalable level. We wanted to move from being a successful niche player to becoming a challenge to the established players.

'When I first approached TTJ, who was still smarting from the HomeShikari debacle, he turned down the idea. However, persistence paid off, and my efforts to convince him on the need to grow synergistically made him and his brother Raghu (both key to any investment from the family kitty) agree to invest. I met TTJ at least five times to discuss this idea over a period of one year. He invested in this software product company, which is working on the cutting edge of technology in the immigration domain.'

Safety net

Sunder describes what has kept him going: 'TTJ always told us he was providing a safety net just in case our parachutes failed. And that is true. He has supported our ventures through thick and thin. When I first entered the Group, I was a rank outsider, but TTJ still valued my opinion. I was just thirty, much younger than my peers in the more established Group companies. I am forty-five now, and still probably the youngest person in the Group who reports to TTJ.

'My financial acumen has probably improved a lot only because of him; he can quickly deduce how the company is doing by just looking at one or two key numbers. He has a phenomenal memory, so it is impossible to bullshit him.

'He has provided me with great freedom to operate the company, keeping in mind the best interests of the clients, the employees and the shareholders. He is non-interfering as far as my business is concerned. But at the same time he has a special affinity towards it because he has also invested in it personally, and not just from the family wealth.

'Whenever I sought his advice on any professional matter concerning Venky during the time he worked with me, TTJ's reply would be, "You talk to him, you are his boss." The younger generation of the family too are very clear about their respective roles as employee or key shareholder or board member. I have always been surprised by their lack of airs and their rare and distinct humility.'

Quirky jobs

TTK Services has performed a variety of tasks for its clients, some rather sensitive and some rather bizarre and unusual.

The concierge service, YourManinIndia, arranged for 365 balloons in the living room of a house in Visakhapatnam at the request of an NRI client to celebrate his wife's birthday.

A poignant request that we complied with was to accompany a Bangalore-based old couple and their mentally disabled son on a temple tour. This request was from their other son in the US.

We had carried out several such remarkable requests, including arranging lunch at a five-star hotel in Chennai for the father of an NRI and taking him to visit his native place in Puducherry for a trip down memory lane.

We handled regular chores for an NRI's parents in Kolkata, right from regular visits to them just to provide them moral support, to buying them groceries and medicines, taking them to the hospital, making utility payments, payments to their maid, and arranging for an air conditioner, TV and fridge in their home.

GetFriday

GetFriday, the virtual assistant (VA) business, also had its share of unusual requests, which ranged from reminding an overzealous client not to speed and collecting parking fines, to collect homework information from a teacher's voicemail and emailing it to the client (parents of the student). Our VAs have also taken up the task of drawing up a diet plan for clients, sending them regular reminders to stick to the plan, and even ordering groceries for the client based on his or her specific diet plan. In one instance, a VA was contacted by a person who needed help in finding a job. Ironically, he had lost his job because of outsourcing. Our VA did a job search, wrote cover letters and drafted the client's resume, getting him a job within thirty days.

From fixing a broken windowpane of a house in Geneva to organizing an event for a magazine in Columbia, it was all handled remotely by the company. Providing evidence for a trial and information on a person missing in a hurricane, our Fridays have done it all.

In 2005, A.J. Jacobs, editor-at-large of *Esquire* magazine, was inspired by Thomas Friedman's *The World Is Flat* to begin a well-documented experiment with GetFriday. He outsourced his personal life to one of our VAs, and the tasks he asked us to do ranged from apologizing to his wife and sending her flowers and cards on his behalf, to reading bedtime stories to his young child on the phone . . . all the way down to buying him underwear!

15

PROFESSIONALS IN CHARGE

Keep the best interests of the business in mind
when you pass on the baton.

I retire as executive chairman of TTK Prestige on 13 May 2018, which will be my seventieth birthday. After I leave, the company will be run by professionals as none of my sons[1] is directly involved in the company. I have groomed the top leadership team of Prestige over the last few years, and we have an excellent professional management in place.

This is not too different from the story at many other business houses. Look at Walmart, for example. Sam Walton started it, but the company is not run by any of his children, though they are all on its board. In India too, quite a few family businesses have transited to becoming professionally run, and have remained successful after the transition.

---

[1] Jagannathan's daughter, Vydehi, died in a car accident in 2004, at the age of twenty.

For example, Asian Paints, Dabur and Marico are all big companies started by families, but they are no longer run by the family members. Asian Paints was started by Choksi, but there is no Choksi running the company today; Dabur was started by Dr Burman, but there's no Burman running the company now. Similarly, Marico was started by Mariwala, but no Mariwala runs the company today. There are more such examples.

There are also instances of the opposite, where businesses continue to be run by family members. At Havells, for instance, Keemat Rai Gupta appointed his son as the managing director; Rahul Bajaj appointed Rajeev Bajaj as head of Bajaj Auto; and Brij Mohan Munjal appointed Pawan Munjal in charge of Hero MotoCorp. These companies have stayed as family-run businesses, and they are successful too. Of course, there are instances of successors ruining businesses too. You can never tell. I would have liked one of my sons to join Prestige, but I have accepted that they won't. I think it's a matter of whether one has the passion for it. If my children had been passionate about the business, they would have got more involved a long time ago. But they haven't been keen on it, just the way I had not been interested in the family business as I didn't think I had the aptitude for it. I joined the business reluctantly because there was no one else who could step in.

A difficult decision

Now, we have groomed professional managers to take charge. My sons will keep an eye on the board and, of course, they will advise the managing director. If he doesn't perform, they'll find another one. I know it's not going to be easy; there are no easy solutions. But what else could I do? What if I nominated one of my sons to become the next managing director and he were to make a mess of it? There would be a lot more difficulty in removing a son than in replacing someone from outside the family. My children are in agreement with me that running the company should be entrusted to professionals. It takes a lot of guts though, to take such a decision.

The retirement age in the company is sixty-five. I'm already past that age. But the board did not want me to retire because we had a new managing director; the previous MD, S. Ravichandran, retired in 2015 after eighteen years in the post, and the board wanted me to stay on for five more years to hand-hold the incumbent MD, and I agreed to stay on until I turned seventy.

When I resign from the board my younger sons can join the board as directors of TTK Prestige. My brother is already on the board, and we can't at present have more than two family members on it, as I am the executive chairman and also a family member. My wife was a director but gave up her place to Mukund, our oldest son, as she believes that it was more important for him to be on the board to maintain continuity of our presence.

Pulse of the company

I still have my finger on the pulse of the company, but I don't interfere with its running. Once a quarter we have an operations meeting when I am briefed about the operations of the company. The meetings last the whole day, from 8 a.m. to 6 p.m. The head of every department makes a presentation to me.

The professionals have gradually begun taking all the decisions. Chandru Kalro is the managing director and has been with TTK Prestige from 1993. K. Shankaran has been the secretary of the company since 1990 and is on the board of TTK Prestige Ltd since 1993.

After I retire from the role of executive chairman, I will continue as chairman. I have informed the board of that and they are in agreement with it. I will keep my office and come here maybe once a week. I will still be watching, so I can help if necessary, but I will retire and give them that space so that when I die they will be able to stand on their own feet. After all, it's just a matter of practice.

Different goals

There is an entrepreneurial instinct in my sons, and each has his own goal.

My eldest son, Mukund, is a scientist, and on the faculty of the National Centre for Biological Sciences (NCBS), a premier research institute located in Bangalore. We knew early on that his interest lay in academics, and I did not want to bring him into the business the way I was brought in.

Dr Mukund Thattai has a BA in physics from Cornell University, a PhD in physics from the Massachusetts Institute of Technology, and has specialized in computational cell biology. He says, 'The issue of coming back to India came up after I completed my PhD and came back to Bangalore for a visit. NCBS had a new programme where you could join directly after your PhD, and I got an offer from them. But I had better offers in the US, and discussed my options with Amma and

Appa. Appa said I should choose Bangalore because the family was here, the business was here and I had a job offer here. He didn't say I had to come back for the business, but he wanted me to be peripherally involved in it. So I accepted the offer from NCBS and set up a synthetic biology lab there. Apart from the research, the job of raising funds for the lab and building a team is very much entrepreneurial.'

My second son, Lakshman, studied mechanical and aerospace engineering in Cornell University. He worked with several companies in the US, including TTK Services, and then ran the Manttra business there until we closed it. He also worked for quite some time in the TTK Food business in India, and came up with innovative products, like the pani puri pellets. He has now started his own venture, Unifize.

Lakshman Thattai says, 'It was great working with my father in the Manttra business. He taught me a lot of things; he taught me how to sell; and he taught me something that he was taught by his father, which is to "never say no to an opportunity". My father never says no when someone wants to meet him. A random person can call his office and ask for an appointment to see him, and he won't refuse. He believes that even if 90 per cent of such meetings are a complete waste of time, 10 per cent would turn out to be something amazing. That's something that I value and practise too. He also has an incredible ability to very quickly spot anomalies or patterns to which other people are completely oblivious; it is quite incredible.

'A few months after I moved back to India, I was offered the opportunity of running the foods division, which is part of TTK Healthcare and which my uncle runs. It had repeatedly struggled, and the company was contemplating selling it, but decided to upgrade the manufacturing facility and renew the business. They needed someone to manage that project of installing very sophisticated machinery, and I was given that opportunity. I very aggressively pushed my responsibility, and after about a year I was running the entire show.

'The first thing that I realized was that I had to be involved. I would always wonder why my father had to get into each and everything the business did. But I learnt that if you don't get involved, you can't set goals for others. I learnt that you had to go in there and challenge every single thing. I started using my mechanical engineering knowledge for the first time. We enhanced manufacturing capacity from 120 tonnes a month to 1000 tonnes a month. We were smart about utilizing the considerable investment, and it paid off.

'The biggest learning for me was how to bring about the best in people and build a team. We did very well; the food division's turnover, when I joined, was Rs 7 crore, and it was Rs 70 crore when I left in April 2016.

'I wanted to take the learnings from here to do something of my own. I'm nearly forty now, and if I am going to do it, this is the time. I'm not a fan of nepotism. At the foods division, I was just another employee and reported to someone two rungs below my uncle. The professionals in Prestige are extremely good, and I respect them a lot.'

My third son, Venkatesh, studied theatre and mathematics at Cornell University and worked for TTK Services here for ten years. He ran GetFriday and HomeShikari, and for a while, he worked in TTK Prestige's water purifier business. He too wanted to do something on his own and has started an art activity centre where people of all ages can take classes and short courses in various arts.

Venkatesh Thattai says, 'Appa never pressured us to join the business, though I think there were a lot of implicit expectations. Unlike standard business family heads who take it for granted that the children would come and start working with them, Appa didn't force anything upon us.

'I returned to India after my BA and taught theatre for a couple of years, but I didn't want to be a teacher all my life. Appa then mentioned the business unit that Sunder was heading, and that interested me.

'When Lakshman and I started working in the Group at different points, Appa put us in charge of things that were not directly under him or were far away enough from him, where we didn't have to interact with each other at home and at work on a daily basis. He's very supportive of us going into our own business ventures and doing our own thing.'

Chandru Kalro, managing director at TTK Prestige since 2015, joined the company in 1993 as a product manager. He says, 'TTJ has a very different leadership style. He leads by example. He doesn't preach one thing and do another. TTJ is larger than life in this company, he cannot tolerate fools and he makes no bones about it. Unless you are in a position to understand what he actually wants, you are going to find it difficult to work with him directly. But if you understand what he wants, you will find that he is an extremely simple person. For example, I was a product manager when I joined, and when I felt that the aesthetic quality of our goods was not good, I would criticize it.

'One day he came to me and said, "I'm going to Chicago for a show, why don't you just come along? See what you like, give me a few benchmarks instead of just criticizing me." Here I am, a man who had never stepped out of India, and suddenly he takes me abroad for no apparent reason. He gave me no work there. All he said was, "Go, look around and tell me what you want." How many people would do that? How many people would invest in an employee who criticizes them?

'He sees the honesty of purpose behind your criticism. I have not worked in many other companies, but I don't think that this kind of culture exists in other companies. I'm not the only one who has stuck around for so long. I have been with TTK Prestige for twenty-four years. You will find people who have been working here for twenty-five and thirty years. TTJ is very accessible and we can walk into his office any time. When he travels with us, he's one of us.

'TTJ is an engineer in his entire approach to life. He is an extremely logical person and brilliant at what he does. Apart from his academic qualifications, he has a very quick mind and has a head for numbers that can surprise most people.

'He is extremely passionate about this company, he lives and breathes it. I have seen him in his office at 10 a.m. a day after he had a surgery that lasted three and a half hours.

'The very strong organizational culture in the Group and the family's own culture are the critical blocks with which the company has been built, and which makes it better than most others.'

K. Shankaran, group director (corporate affairs) at TTK Group, says, 'I struck a good rapport with Mr Jagannathan and I found a home in the TTK Group. As far as I am concerned, he treats me as a leader. He spots the right persons and trusts them, and a professional is willing to perform when this happens. It takes him just an hour to build trust in you, and after that you can be sure that he will always be with you, whether your advice and decisions are right or wrong.

'He handed over to me the final say in all tax matters and trusted me enough to work with both central and state governments on policies. I was appointed the convener of the Pressure Cooker Industry Association.

'The most interesting role that I had was to deal with the trade unions. There were six unions in our two factories and they often struck work. Over a period of eight months, in 2002–03, I held fifty-six meetings with the six unions and got them to merge into a single union. The increase in the wage bill was 10 per cent, while the increase in productivity was 40 per cent. We became operationally economical. The team which led this company to rise like a phoenix from the ashes is still there, and the spirit is still there. Even when we all retire, that spirit will be there.'

16

A SOCIAL CONSCIENCE

Philanthropy includes devoting time and energy,
along with money, to causes.

In 1979, my older brother, Ranganathan, died of alcoholism at the age of thirty-two. It was painful to watch him slide into the clutches of addiction. At that time, addiction was not acknowledged as a disease and there were no treatment centres in India.

We took him first to England and then to the USA for treatment. He recovered and came back to India, but later died of pancreatitis.

Deeply affected by this, his wife, Shanthi, was determined to spread awareness about alcoholism as a disease. She trained at the Hazelden Institute in Minneapolis, USA, and returned to Chennai to set up the T.T. Ranganathan Clinical Research Foundation with my father's support.

A community approach

Interpreting addiction as a 'community problem' instead of a personal problem, the Foundation, which manages the TTK Hospital, has successfully treated and rehabilitated more than 40,000 alcoholics and drug addicts, many of them for free.

Supported by the TTK Group, which provided the initial investment of Rs 1 crore to buy 48,000 sq. ft of land in Indira Nagar in Chennai, the Foundation has grown into one of the pioneer centres in the field of de-addiction. The hospital and rehabilitation centre has a picturesque 33,000 sq. ft campus. It has established standards of treatment and care that are followed by 400 centres all over India and Asia.

International collaborations

The Foundation collaborates with the International Labour Organisation and the United Nations Drug Control Programme to conduct training programmes, workshops and awareness drives in various industries and institutions. It also reaches out to the community and conducts awareness camps in villages.

The Foundation also imparts training under the Colombo Plan, UNODC and, under the aegis of the Government of India, training to social workers, nurses, doctors, psychologists and other interested people from all over India and parts of Asia.

My sister-in-law, Shanthi, has been awarded the Padma Shri, the fourth highest civilian award in the country, by the President of India in 1992 for her service. She was also the first recipient of the United Nations Vienna Civil Society Award for Outstanding Contributions in the Fight against Drug Abuse in

1999. She was awarded the Avvaiyar Award by the government of Tamil Nadu in 2015.

Shanthi now lives in Manjakudi, a village near Kumbakonam, where she administers a technical institute that follows the principles of Swami Dayananda Saraswati. The institute imparts technical training in various engineering fields to students as an alternative to formal school education. We have given a support of Rs 1 crore to the institute.

My cousin Varadu's wife, Maya Varadarajan, has taken up the management of the TTK hospital in an honorary capacity after Shanthi retired from active work at the hospital.

Not just money, but time and energy

Even in the years that we struggled, Mother insisted that we give one-sixth of our income to social causes. We have been doing so diligently, and the TTK Group has the unique distinction of being a pioneer in the social sector. Much before corporate social responsibility (CSR) became a buzzword and the government made it mandatory for companies to take up CSR, we have been supporting very important causes.

Apart from the de-addiction centre for alcoholics and drug addicts, some of the social projects to which the Group and our family members dedicate energy, time and money to are blood banks, a bone bank, a stem cell donor registry, and support to critical research and development in science.

Rotary Bangalore–TTK Blood Bank

My wife, Dr Latha Jagannathan, was instrumental in setting up the Bangalore Medical Services Trust (BMST) in 1984, and the Rotary–TTK Blood Bank, which is under the aegis of the Trust, and saves nearly one lakh lives every year. It is one of the largest regional blood transfusion centres and blood component facilities in Karnataka. TTK Prestige has been donating Rs 50,000 to Rs 1 crore per year to this activity.

Latha is a trained medical doctor. On learning about the shortage of blood that was affecting patients in Bangalore, and inspired by the work of her cousin Shanthi Ranganathan in Chennai, she, with her friends Malathi Aiyar and Lalli Srimurthy, began organizing voluntary blood donation camps and motivated people to donate blood to hospitals in Bangalore. The Rotary Club of Bangalore approached them to set up a blood bank, and this led to the establishment of BMST.

Initially set up to provide blood-banking services through its division, Rotary Bangalore–TTK Blood Bank, BMST has evolved over time to become a centre of excellence in the areas of blood banking, transfusion, immunohematology, transplant immunology, tissue banking, solid organ and stem cell transplantation, training, research and community-based health education and health services.

Latha later trained in tissue matching and typing at Hoxworth Blood Center, University of Cincinnati, Ohio, and BMST is the sole standalone NGO in India which has a blood bank, tissue bank, HLA Lab and stem cell registry, and is therefore able to provide a wide spectrum of services in the field of blood, organ and cellular therapies.

BMST used to function out of the offices of the TTK Group till 1990. In 1991 it received a grant of land from the government of Karnataka in Thippasandra, Bangalore. Today, it has a voluntary donor base of over five lakh, who donate almost 40,000 units of blood per year at blood donation camps held in over 600 IT industries, colleges, universities and other organizations.

Both Latha, who is the medical director and managing trustee, and Lakshmi Ravichandran (the wife of our former MD), trustee at BMST and head, donor recruitment, have volunteered their time, effort and expertise to establish and grow BMST into what it is today. Latha received the 'Citizen Extraordinaire' award from the Rotary Club of Bangalore in 2005.

Madras Voluntary Blood Bank

The Madras Voluntary Blood Bank was initiated more than forty years ago by my eldest sister-in-law, Shanthi, and this was taken over by my brother Raghu's wife, Bhanu Raghunathan. In addition to managing MVBB, she also set up the Rotary Central-VHS-TTK blood bank in Chennai.

Education, health and nutrition

The TTK Group supports projects of other public charitable trusts in education, health and nutrition. We support the Nandalala Seva Samithi Trust, which has set up a public library in a rural area near Puducherry; the Bhuvana Foundation, which educates tribal children; and the Jungle Escapes Charitable Trust for Forest and Ecological Preservation. We support some scientific projects of Tata Institute of Sciences and also a project to encourage children to take up space studies.

We have provided machinery for a low-cost dialysis centre in Chennai and help the Mayaa Foundation for treatment for children born with facial deformities.

Apart from helping Mathruseva in feeding the needy, we support the Karnataka State Council for Child Welfare's project for provision of mid-day meals to children.

Humanities chair

I wanted to institute a chair in my alma mater, IIT Madras, and Mother suggested that it be in the humanities. When I was a student there, IIT had a five-year course, and English was compulsory in the first two years, as were history and German. The curriculum was narrowed after it became a four-year course. Mother felt that students who study science and engineering need to be exposed to the humanities, and we instituted the TTK Chair in the humanities.

R2D2

We also support the Rehabilitation Research and Device Development Lab at IIT Madras, which is involved in research related to human movement, the influence of orthotic and prosthetic devices on human movement, and the design and development of mechanisms, products and assistive devices for people with impairments.

Dr Sujatha Srinivasan of the department of mechanical engineering in IIT Madras is a very smart person. After doing her PhD in prosthetics, she had worked for a company in the US and realized that knees made in the West were not transferable to India. Apart from the higher cost, some of the activities that are intrinsically Indian, such as squatting or sitting cross-legged, are not possible with a knee made for Westerners.

It had to be done differently for India, and Sujatha set up a centre in IIT Madras, of which she is an alumna. The director was very pleased with the project, but it needed a lot of money. Sujatha came to meet me and made a presentation, and I agreed to support them; we have given Rs 3.8 crore over three years towards the project.

The TTK Center for Rehabilitation Research and Device Development (R2D2) was inaugurated in January 2015. I am delighted that the researchers at the centre have been winning several design patents for their inventions.

Science without boundaries

More recently, we helped the Bangalore Life Science Cluster's 'Science without Boundaries' project with a funding support of Rs 3 crore. The Bangalore Life Science Cluster comprises three premier research institutions: National Centre for Biological Sciences, NCBS-TIFR (a centre of Tata Institute of Fundamental Research), Institute for Stem Cell Biology and Regenerative Medicine (inStem) and Centre for Cellular and Molecular Platforms (CCAMP).

Several early-career researchers, investigators, visiting scientists and international experts work together at the Cluster to address diverse research questions that range from nanotechnology to ecology and stem cell biology. Global partnerships have been among the key drivers of research at the Cluster. They have helped build capacity and drive multi-institutional programmes. Lack of funds had severely curtailed these programmes.

I believe that science is our only hope to improve the lives of millions of people and that our scientists need to engage with their peers in other countries. We signed an agreement in September 2017 that will strengthen global engagements for research and training.

This initiative came about after I was invited by Dr Kiran Mazumdar Shaw, chairman and managing director of biotechnology major Biocon, and Mr Kris Gopalakrishnan, co-founder of Infosys, to attend a thematic learning session on science and research at the Bangalore Life Science Cluster campus by the India Philanthropy Initiative. It was a workshop for philanthropists to engage in discussions relating to private support for research and innovation.

Prof. Satyajit Mayor, director, NCBS and inStem, acknowledging a donation that the company has made, said: 'This extraordinarily generous donation from TTK Prestige will serve to transform our ability to interact with the ever-widening world of science that we inhabit. It is in these areas that flexibility of functioning has become extremely curtailed in the recent years. This vital and timely support will enable us to regain our capacity for competitive research, and attract the best talent from near and far to engage with our campus.'

Shanthi Ranganathan says about TTJ, 'Jaggu is a great believer in the Almighty. He is also very generous and spontaneous. Apart from visiting Tirupati, he also used to visit Thiruvallur to pay obeisance to the family deity, and on one such visit he found a number of pilgrims sleeping by the roadside. He immediately arranged for a *choultry* (boarding house) to be constructed for pilgrims.'

R.H. Krishna Murthy, who has been Jagannathan's confidential secretary from 1975, says, 'TTJ is a very demanding boss but a caring human being. Some years ago, when my arteries were blocked, he sent me to his own doctor and arranged for my treatment. When I was hospitalized, he went to Tirupati and came straight to the hospital with the prasad. I was very moved when he touched my leg to see if there was a pulse. Not only that, he had taken a vow that he would take me to Tirupati whenever he visited and did so nearly every month, for almost ten years. I look up to him as an elder brother.'

17

THE KARMA OF BUSINESS

It is the karma of a businessman to run a successful business.

Do I consider myself a lucky person? Yes and no. When Napoleon wanted to pick one of five generals to lead a battle, his advisers suggested the names of those who had won previous wars. Napoleon said, 'Tell me who is the luckiest. That's whom I want.' You need to have luck, and, fortunately, I have had it.

Let me give you some examples of luck. Paytm, the electronic payment company, was struggling for six years until the government demonetized the rupee in 2016. Paytm's business has now grown to such an extent that *Time* magazine listed its founder, Vijay Shekhar Sharma, on the 2017 *Time* 100, the publication's annual list of the 100 most influential people in the world. Is that luck or isn't that luck?[1]

---

[1]   Nilekani, Nandan. 'The 100 Most Influential People.' *Time*. time.com/collection/2017-time-100/4742761/vijay-shekhar-sharma/

Similarly, Sunil Bharti Mittal, whom I used to know very well, got lucky. He was in the right place and at the right time. We were both in manufacturing. I was making pressure cookers, while he was making landline telephones. He started by making a telephone called Beetel in Ludhiana, which was not a very big product. When the government opened up the telecom industry and invited applications for licences, he moved from manufacturing to telecom services. He didn't invent the mobile phone, but by moving from manufacturing to providing mobile telephone services, he grew Bharti Airtel into a global telecommunications company. That's great timing.

On the other hand, there was a phone manufacturer here in Bangalore who was even bigger than Beetel and had a Swedish collaboration. This company died because it was just making landline telephones and could not survive in the world of mobile telephony.

A different kind of luck

I didn't have the kind of luck that Sharma and Mittal did, but I have had luck of a different kind, which has included a combination of logic, blessings and self-belief.

I had luck in the sense that I followed logic and did the right things accordingly. Now, that doesn't necessarily lead to success. If luck is not with you, everything can fail.

The most important factor in my success was my parents' blessings. My father supported all my decisions. If I felt depressed, I would go talk to my mother and she would say, 'You will pull it around, Jaggu. Don't worry. I know you will pull it around.' The blessings of my parents have seen me through.

When Hanuman was entrusted with the task of finding Sita, he wondered how he would make it across the sea to Lanka. Jambavan told him, 'You don't know this, but if you leap, you can cross the sea.' Similarly, my mother used to tell me constantly, 'You can do it,' and I was able to do what I did.

God and karma

Somebody once asked me if I was a spiritual person. I find it hard to define the word 'spiritual'. I believe in God. I am not a great one for rituals, pujas and *homams*, but I certainly believe in God and I believe in the theory of karma. Somewhere, karma kicks in.

I rationalize that, good or not, everything happens because of it. Karma is what you have done; it can't be changed but it can be mitigated by doing good things. I don't particularly do any good things because I don't do any bad things. In our religion we don't have tombstones, but if I were to have one I would like it to read, 'He didn't harm anyone.' That's all. I won't claim that I have done a lot of good, but I have employed 20,000 people and have never reneged on paying their salary, not even for a day. That's my share of good.

I think that it is the karma of the businessman to run a successful business. Except that I am an accidental businessman.

Patience

I am an extrovert and I like people, but I am not always cheerful. As a Gemini, I have two facets to my personality. When disaster strikes I get depressed. I go into a shell and start thinking about how to solve the problem. I go home and don't speak to anybody. I watch TV and play cards while trying to figure out a solution. I play two hours of Patience every day, I play for an hour in the morning before I read the newspaper, and for another hour in the evening. I play ten different kinds of solitaire.

I enjoy playing Blackjack and have had memorable wins at casinos. My final paper in Cornell in probability theory was on Blackjack. After the exams I went to Las Vegas and won a ton of money playing Blackjack. Another time, when we were holidaying with a group of friends and families, all our money was stolen at the airport in Nairobi. Those were the days before credit cards, and all we had was mostly cash. I went to a casino and won a handsome amount.

Never accept defeat

I never accept defeat, be it in business or in a sport. This is what spurred me to take up golf. I had once accompanied a very close friend, Dr Srimurthy, to the golf course in Ooty. He is a very good player, and when I walked along with him for three holes, I said, 'This is very easy. Give me one of those sticks, I can also play this game.' It was heresy. I put the ball on the ground but I couldn't even touch it, though I took ten shots at it. I was very irritated that I could not hit a stationary ball, and it had no spin or googly, unlike a cricket ball.

I was taken aback as sports came naturally to me. I had played tennis for India as a junior. We had a tennis court at home, and I had started to play when I was ten. When I was fifteen, my contemporaries were Vijay Amritraj, who is three years younger than me, and Anand Amritraj, who is a year younger than me. The three of us had the same coach, Ramarao. I was playing very good tennis until the coach changed my grip from my natural flat hand to the shake hand that was popular those days. I could not get used to the new grip and my game was destroyed. I did not play at the professional level after that, though I captained the tennis team at IIT. Today, ironically, everybody plays with my grip, but that's how life can be sometimes.

I could not accept my inability to play golf and decided that I had to learn to play this game. I became a corporate member of the Bangalore Golf Club, bought a set of clubs and started playing by myself. I refused coaching and developed a very unorthodox style. But I enjoyed the game and used to play two rounds nearly every day of the week. It has been five years since I played, though, as I have fibrosis of the lung, which makes it difficult to walk for long. I had taken up golf thinking I could play it until I was ninety. In recent years, I have switched to my old passion, bridge. I play bridge three times a week, mostly at tournaments in various clubs in Bangalore.

Three simple rules of business

I don't go around giving lectures or advice. I refuse invitations to address management students, but now seems like a good time to say a few words about my learnings in running a business. I would not venture to advise anyone setting up a business today about the nature of their business. Today's conditions are so different. Every start-up is digitally based, and I belong to old business. But the rules of running a business would be the same.

It's good to have an MBA, but you don't need a business degree to run a business. After all, the MBA is a recent phenomenon. Vanderbilt, Rockefeller, Carnegie, Kennedy, J.P. Morgan—none of them had an MBA degree. If you take a look at the founders of Flipkart, Big Bazaar, Ola—none of them are MBAs either, and they have done a great job.

I have three simple rules for running a business:

1. Get down to the office every day.
2. Look at the details. Don't see the big picture, look at the small picture. The big picture will look after itself.
3. Apply your common sense, and not just what you read in textbooks.

It's important that you get to work every day and you look at the details, because it's in the detail where you lose money. You only have to look at our business to see how things can go wrong if one looks only at the big picture. My father started businesses that were great. The big picture was fantastic, it was in the detail that it went wrong and in the way everything was executed.

You need acumen and a lot of common sense. You must not be afraid to apply your common sense. It's largely the elementary things that work. When I came up with the GRS for the pressure cooker, all I invented was just a hole in the lid. But the company would have gone bankrupt if not for that hole in the lid. All it took was common sense to fix the problem.

Get to work every day, look at the details, and use a lot of common sense, the most uncommon trait of all.

A legacy

These rules have helped me put the TTK Group and all the businesses in the conglomerate on a sound footing.

They have helped me steer our flagship TTK Prestige's growth from a single factory to five factories, twenty-three warehouses, multiple innovation centres and a network of 50,000 retailers across India. We have an international presence through supplies to Original Equipment Manufacturers (OEMs) in the UK, Europe, US, west Asia, Africa, south-east Asia, Australia and New Zealand.

In 2003, TTK Prestige was worth about Rs 100 crore; in 2013, it was worth Rs 1300 crore. We became one of the most admired companies in the stock market too. Our share price initially shot up to Rs 4000 and then continued to rise. It has been averaging over Rs 6500 this year (April 2017 onwards) and at times, nearing Rs 8000. The company's market capital now exceeds Rs 8000 crore. These numbers power our growth and motivate us to keep innovating and expanding.

We are now the number one brand in both pressure cookers and cookware. We are the only Indian company to offer the complete induction-cooking solution. We are also the number one brand in value-added gas stoves, and we are India's largest kitchen appliance company. What is gratifying is my certainty that you will find a Prestige product in each of the nearly 300 million households in India.

Had I started my journey as a businessman with zero capital, I would have been ten times richer than I am now, but I began with a colossal deficit. There has never been a dull moment on this journey. I fulfilled my father's desire to pay off the Group's debts, built a sound foundation for the business that has been in the family for three generations, and I am leaving it in the secure hands of professionals. I have enjoyed the risks I took and the disruptions I caused along the way. This is the true measure of my success as I get ready to hang up my boots.

ACKNOWLEDGEMENTS

The idea for this book came from a talk that T.T. Jagannathan gave at the annual Ayaz Peerbhoy Memorial Lecture in January 2017. To say that I found the talk very engaging would be an understatement. His genuine passion for his work and his justifiable pride were impressive. His account of the many problems of the business and their turnarounds were pretty hair-rising.

When I broached the idea of this book, I was not very sure if TTJ would agree to it, but my theory in life is that an answer can't be worse than a 'no'. My optimism was rewarded as, after hearing me out, TTJ said, 'I have never done anything like this before and I am curious about the process. If you think anybody would be interested in reading such a book, I am willing to be interviewed.'

We started in right earnest, and after several months of interviews with TTJ, his family and current and former colleagues in different cities, the result is this book. I am grateful to all of them for their trust and time, and especially to Latha Jagannathan and T.T. Raghunathan for adding depth to the story.

I would like to thank my old friend Melissa Arulappan
for planting the idea of this book in my head, Bunty Peerbhoy
for being the catalyst, Radhika Marwah at Penguin Random
House India for her faith in the project, Marcelle Symms for
transcribing the bulk of the interviews, my extraordinary friends
and family Capt. S. Seshadri, Aditya Mendonca, Subhalakshmi
Roy and Vidya Jois, for being my sounding board and more.

My thanks to historian S. Muthaiah for giving me a copy of
his book *The Man Who Could Never Say No* on T.T. Vasu, and
to Margaret Herdeck and Gita Piramal, the authors of *India's
Industrialists*. Both these books have provided context to some
of the historic events.

Sandhya Mendonca